BLACKWORK EMBROIDERY
IN COLOUR

First published in 2023

Search Press Limited
Wellwood, North Farm Road,
Tunbridge Wells, Kent TN2 3DR

ISBN: 978-1-78221-845-6
ebook ISBN: 978-1-78126-800-1

The projects in this book have been made using metric measurements, and the imperial equivalents provided have been calculated following standard conversion practices. The imperial measurements are often rounded to the nearest ¼in for ease of use, except in rare circumstances; however, if you need more exact measurements, there are a number of excellent online converters that you can use. Always use either imperial or metric measurements, not a combination of both.

Suppliers
For details of suppliers, please visit the Search Press website: www.searchpress.com

Extra copies of the charts are also available to download free from the Bookmarked Hub:
www.bookmarkedhub.com
Search for this book by title or ISBN: the files can be found under 'Book Extras'. Membership of the Bookmarked online community is free.

You are invited to visit more of the author's work:
Author's website: www.tometlilycreations.com
Subscription website: www.broderieandcolourbox.com
Facebook: tometlilycreations
Instagram: @tometlilycreations

Keep in touch with Melanie at tometlily@hotmail.com

DEDICATION

This book is dedicated to all my lovely customers from over the years who make my job such a joy every day. Have fun stitching these new patterns and I look forward to seeing your projects take shape!

THANK YOU

I wanted to take this opportunity to thank all the people that helped me in writing this book.

First of all to Katie from Search Press, who reached out and gave me the opportunity to design and write a book about blackwork in colour and share my passion with you all.

I would also like to especially thank May and Carrie for all their help, guidance and patience answering all my questions! It was a pleasure to create this book with you both.

Thank you to my husband Gilles and our children, Tom and Lily, for their input and advice about the designs.

A big thank you to all the stitchers who lent a helping hand to help me stitch some of the designs in the book. I wouldn't have been able to do it all myself. Véronique, Joëlle, Josie, Janet, Marie-Lise and Candice.

Thanks also go to Pili for sponsoring me with the stitchable items, to Sylvie for her help with technical instructions and my Aunt Jessy for all her help and support.

Thanks to the team at Search Press and also to Stacy Grant, who did a great job on the photos!

BLACKWORK EMBROIDERY
IN COLOUR

A COLOURFUL MODERN TWIST ON A TRADITIONAL TECHNIQUE

MELANIE COUFFE

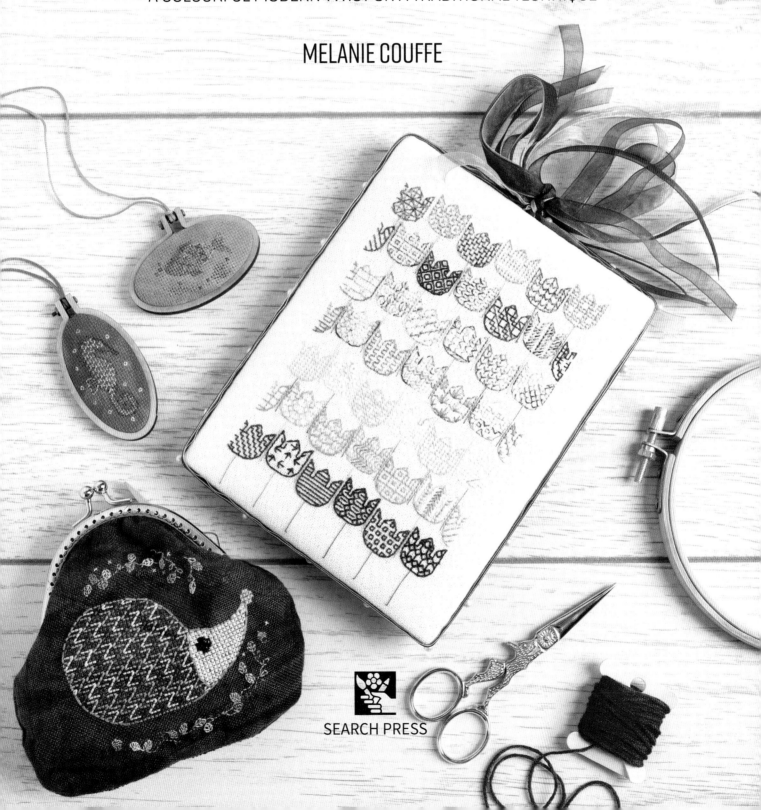

SEARCH PRESS

CONTENTS

SPRING

INTRODUCTION

I'm going to tell you the funny story about how I managed to manifest this book *Blackwork Embroidery in Colour*.

I had the pleasure of having a stand at the Handmade Fair in 2018 at Hampton Court, along with plenty of amazing designers and the Search Press team. Their stand was in the same marquee as mine, and every time I walked past I said to myself, in my mind – I'm going to write a book with you and it'll be called *Blackwork in Colour*. I must have repeated it four or five times over the weekend, but then didn't give it a second thought as I packed everything up and flew back home to France.

A week later I received an email from Katie, the Editorial Director at the time, in which she told me that herself and a colleague, May, had been past my stand and admired my work, and that they would love me to write a book called *Blackwork Embroidery in Colour* for them! Isn't that amazing! It was truly meant to be and here I am today writing the last piece of this book and it's the Introduction!

On my website and social media pages I state that I'm a 'Provider of Joy and Happiness through Colour and Embroidery', and this book is the ideal opportunity for me to do just that. I hope that the designs and choice of colours convey joy and pleasure, and that you are able to enjoy some time to treat yourself to doing something you love.

I love to design by season as this inspires many themes in my work and the different colour combinations fascinate me. You'll find four easy-to-follow sections in this book, themed after the seasons.

Just a last quick note about colour... have fun with it and follow your intuition when choosing your threads and fabric. If you trust yourself and are attracted to certain colours, don't be afraid or worry what other people will think about your choices. The important thing is to have fun and to enjoy the process.

I really hope that the designs in this book bring you as much pleasure and joy as they did me in creating them for you.

Have fun stitching!

HISTORY OF BLACKWORK

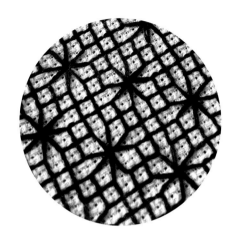

The technique of blackwork embroidery became popular in England during the reign of King Henry VIII (1509–1547), whose first wife, Catherine of Aragon, brought the tradition with her from Spain. At the time she influenced fashion by adding black embroidery to her own clothes, collars, sleeves and cuffs – and even those of King Henry VIII! Originally, this embroidery was done using black silk thread on white linen, and this gave the technique the name 'blackwork'. The intention was to create patterns that looked like intricate lace, so blackwork became known as 'poor people's lace' as it offered a cheaper way to embellish clothes, curtains, cushions and other home accessories.

The embroidery was as pretty on the front as on the back, thanks to Holbein stitch, more commonly known today as double running stitch. The other main stitches used in blackwork were backstitch, stem stitch and chain stitch. Traditional blackwork patterns were created with geometric shapes using backstitch, which added dimension and texture to the stitching.

Nowadays blackwork can be worked with cotton or silk threads and with many different colours. It is usually embroidered on evenweave or aida fabric but it looks great on linen too. Make sure to choose a very regular weave for your fabric – the fabric needs to be the exact same number of warp and weft threads per centimetre/inch.

Blackwork can be used alone or mixed with cross stitch to make pretty embroidery with different textures. It's a fabulous technique to learn as it is easy to do, and is very rewarding thanks to the speed at which you will progress. Once you start blackwork embroidery you won't be able to stop!

GEOMETRIC PATTERNS

Part of the beauty and attraction of blackwork for me is the amazing plethora of geometric patterns that exist for filling in your blackwork embroidery designs.

Working in repetitive geometrical shapes help your brain to relax and produce feel-good hormones as you stitch, bringing a true sense of well-being during the process which continues even after you've put your work away.

There are very simple and easy-to-read stitch patterns, which are ideal for beginners, slightly more complicated ones, right up to extremely intricate ones – all of them more beautiful than the last!

I love to give the geometric beauty of blackwork an extra dimension by adding different colours and playing with the shapes and tones to embellish my stitching further.

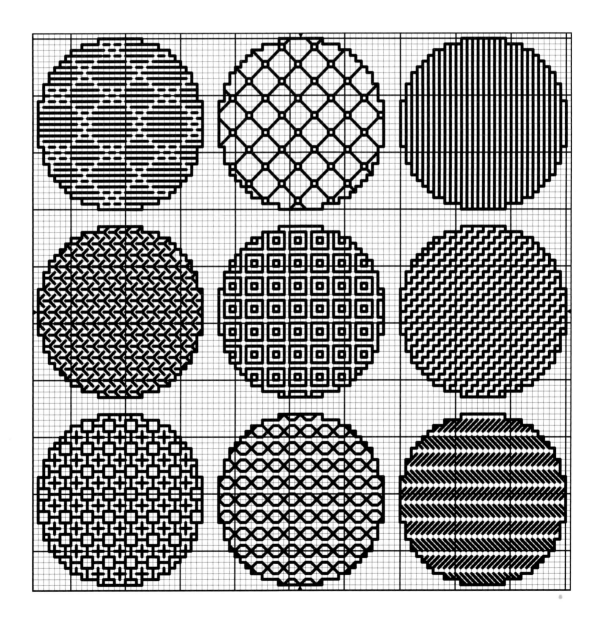

There are two main stages in a blackwork design: first, the outline, which is created using the stitching techniques on pages 16–17, then the geometric filling patterns. The really special thing about these geometric patterns is that you can create your own and adapt them to any shape or contour you like.

Some of my favourite patterns are shown below. They are all stitched using backstitches. They start off quite simply and get more and more intricate as they go on. You could stitch these circular designs to practise if you wish, using the charts opposite (see pages 22–23 for more on reading charts).

COLOUR

Although I love the traditional black-on-white patterns, they were missing something for me. I wanted to create some designs using blackwork geometric patterns, but add a more modern, youthful twist to them. I found the answer with colour. I have an intense relationship with colour, thanks to generations of artists, seamstresses and art school teachers specializing in colour in my family. It is an integral part of me and also the DNA of my business.

The healing power of colour is becoming more widely recognized and a great deal of research has been conducted into each colour's property and the ability to calm, cure and help people feel better in the stressful lives they lead. I recently trained and qualified as a chromotherapist. It has been one of my dreams: to take colour and use it to help others feel healthy and happy.

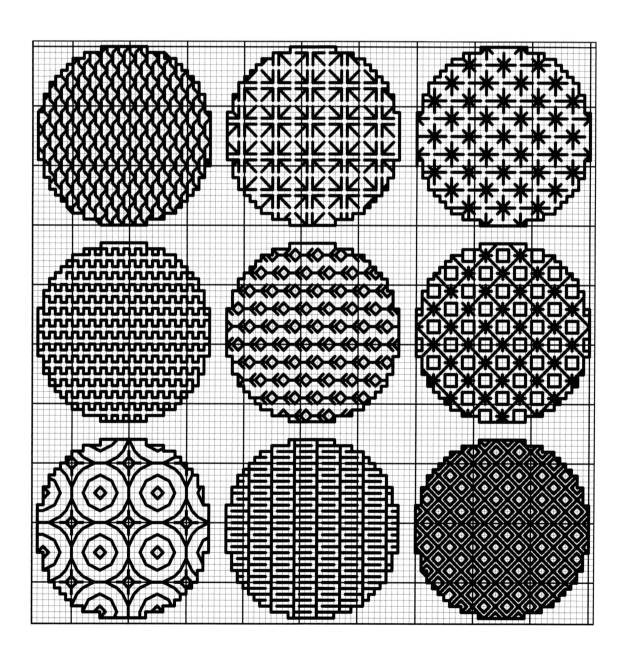

When I create a design and embroider it, hand paint a thread or dye a piece of fabric, I receive the vibrations from the colours that I'm working on at the time, and this has become part of my daily wellness routine. I couldn't keep up the energy required to run my business without it!

Colour makes me feel alive and full of energy and this is what I try and put into my designs, fabrics and threads. I put joy and love into all my products so that they make you feel special when you use them.

My motto is 'colour is life'.

TOOLS AND MATERIALS

THREADS

In this book I've mainly used the thread range Le Fil Atalie, which consist of subtly hand-dyed cotton threads. I have also used several of my Colour Gems threads, which are more vibrant. Both thread ranges are available to buy from my website. I used variegated threads from the CRéAdeS range in a few of my designs. These threads are hand-dyed in Brittany, France, by my friend Adeline Cras. DMC 310 (black) is also used in a couple of the designs. I use cotton sewing thread and strong linen sewing thread to assemble the finished projects.

STITCHING FABRIC

I have mostly used my Tom & Lily Creations hand-dyed stitching fabrics in various colours and the following size types: 20-count aida, 28-count sparkly evenweave, 32-count evenweave, 32-count linen and 32-count sparkly linen. You can buy these from my website, or substitute them for your own choices, but remember to choose the same stitch count for the same sized finished result. For several of the designs I opted for Zweigart 32-count murano evenweave and Zweigart 32-count linen, which are widely available online and in craft stores.

EMBROIDERY HOOPS

Wooden or plastic embroidery hoops are used to keep your stitching fabric taut while you embroider on it. They're very fashionable at the moment as simple but effective frames for your work once finished. I used several different sized wooden embroidery hoops in this book, including the mini ones for the Marine jewellery on page 52. Hoops are widely available in craft stores and online.

NEEDLES

Blackwork embroidery requires a blunt-ended tapestry needle. The size depends on the thread count of your chosen fabric. I have a preference for either John James or Bohin tapestry needles in size 26 for when I work on 28-count and 32-count linen or evenweave, or size 24 when I'm stitching on 20-count aida.

SCISSORS

Use embroidery scissors for snipping your threads and fabric scissors for trimming your fabric and wadding/batting.

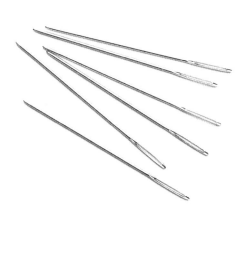

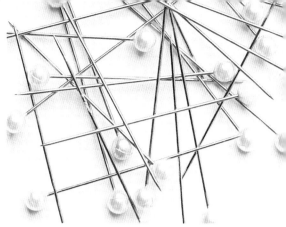

OTHER ITEMS

STICKY TAPE

Both masking tape and double-sided sticky tape are really handy when assembling your work.

WADDING/BATTING

I used cotton wadding/batting to assemble the finished projects, in particular when attaching the backing to projects in hoops (see pages 20–22 for more on this).

RIBBONS

I love finishing off some of my designs with a simple cluster of organza ribbons in several different colours that complement the finished design.

BUTTONS

Buttons can add a decorative finishing touch to your embroidered projects. I've used them for the Biscornu (pages 38–40) and Pumpkin citrolli (pages 64–67).

PINS

I use regular sewing pins to help assemble the finished projects. I also use pearl-headed pins for decorating projects such as the Tulip pinkeep (see page 30) and the Pumpkin citrolli (see page 64).

IRON-ON FABRIC ADHESIVE

This can be bought in a roll or a sheet, and is used for the Hedgehog purse on page 68.

TOTE BAG

I used a hand-dyed cotton tote bag for the Flamingo tote bag on page 48. These are available to order from my website.

STITCHABLE PHONE CASES

For the mobile phone case designs on page 56, I used stitchable cases for smart phones that I bought online.

PURSE CLASP

I used a purse clasp (pictured on the left) for the Hedgehog purse on page 68. They are widely available online and in craft stores.

CANDLE HOLDERS

For the Foliage trio project on page 76, I used three decorative candle holders from a homeware store. You could use any dish or frame of your choice with an inside diameter of 12cm (4¾in).

SEWING MACHINE

I used a sewing machine for the Hedgehog purse on page 68 and Flamingo tote bag on page 48, but you could always hand-sew these if you don't have a machine.

IRON

You will want to iron your embroidery flat. Always do this very carefully on the back of the work.

STITCH GUIDE

BASIC STITCHES USED IN BLACKWORK EMBROIDERY

To keep things easy and straightforward, I have mostly used the backstitch technique (see below) for all of my patterns in this book. As every design is made into an object or a finished flat piece, the back doesn't show and doesn't have to be 100 per cent perfect.

For perfect blackwork stitching as pretty and regular on the front as on the back, you could use more sophisticated techniques like double running stitch (sometimes called Holbein stitch). Chain stitch and stem stitch are also often used in traditional blackwork embroidery work to create shape and form, but won't be used in this book for simplicity.

Backstitch

Backstitch is the most commonly used and the most basic stitch that I use in the patterns in this book. It is very versatile and can be used for both straight and curved lines. It is also the easiest stitch to use for outlining a shape and symmetrical filling patterns in blackwork, being less heavy than chain stitch or stem stitch. We often use this stitch in cross stitch embroidery to delineate subjects or to accentuate part of our work. I'm sure you use it all the time!

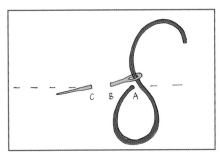 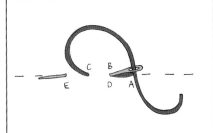 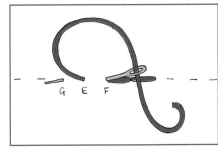

1 Bring the needle up through the fabric at A and pull the thread through. Insert the needle at B and bring it up at C. Pull the thread through the fabric.

2 Insert the needle at D and bring it up through the fabric at E. Pull the thread through.

3 Insert the needle at F and bring it up through the fabric at G. Continue working along the stitch line until it is completed. To finish off, thread your needle through the stitches on the back of your work.

You can create so many interesting shapes with backstitch.

Notice the lovely colour variation created on these tulips using my hand-dyed variegated threads (see Tulip pinkeep, pages 30–33).

Double running stitch/Holbein stitch

Double running stitch is a specific stitch for blackwork embroidery. It can be used to embroider curtains, shirt collars and cuffs, and other items where we can see both sides of the fabric. It is similar to backstitch to look at, but needs a slightly different technique to stitch it – working in one direction outlines the shape, and working back in the opposite way fills in the gaps. This creates a line of solid stitching that looks the same on both sides. This stitch allows the embroidery to be as neat on the back as on the front of your embroidery fabric.

I Begin stitching as in step I of backstitch (see opposite), but continue to make evenly spaced stitches with gaps in between. Bring the needle up in the first hole of the last stitch.

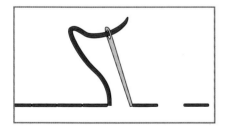

2 Without turning your fabric, make a stitch over the first gap, and continue to fill in the gaps in the same way.

Tacking/basting stitch

Tacking/basting is used to hold fabric together temporarily and keep the pieces in place while you work on them. It's made with long stitches, usually in a contrasting coloured thread, and is removed once the work is finished.

Cross stitch

In this book I have added some cross stitches to the blackwork to give some depth to my designs. Made up of simple 'X' shaped stitches, they can be used to fill areas, as an outline or just for decoration.

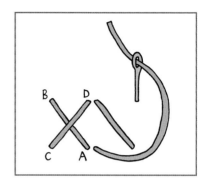

Bring the needle up through the fabric at A and insert it at B to create one half of your cross. Bring the needle up at C and then take it down at D to complete.

Whipstitch

This is a technique that is used to join pieces of stitched fabric together. When used in this book, I fold the fabric pieces along a line of backstitch and the two lines of backstitching are brought together and stitched through.

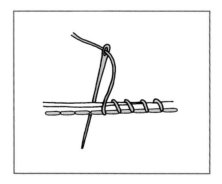

I Place the two sides of the fabric together so that the backstitches sit against each other horizontally.

2 Pass your needle and thread through two backstitches from top to bottom, without passing through the fabric itself. Keep repeating this for each pair of backstitches going from right to left.

TECHNIQUES

USING AN EMBROIDERY HOOP

It isn't necessary to use an embroidery hoop when stitching blackwork designs, but it will help to keep your fabric taut and your stitching neat and tidy.

1 Fold your piece of fabric in four in order to find the centre. (If there is a stitch at the centre of the chart you can make your first stitch at this point.)

2 Loosen the clasp on the hoop and separate both parts.

3 Place the inner (smaller) hoop on a flat surface. Centre your fabric over the inner hoop and place the outer (larger) hoop on top of the fabric and smaller hoop. Push down over both. Pull and adjust your fabric so that it's taut.

4 Tighten the clasp on the outer hoop to secure everything in place.

STARTING YOUR STITCHING

Familiarize yourself with the relevant chart before you start stitching. Find the centre of the chart (see 'Reading a blackwork embroidery chart' on pages 22–23). If there are no stitches at the centre, find the next closest stitch and count the number of squares or stitches from the centre to this stitch on your chart, then do the same on your fabric.

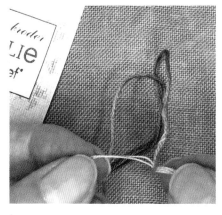

TIPS

I like to take a metre (1yd) length of two strands of the thread I'm using and cut it in half to work with 50cm (19¾in) lengths. This is easier to stitch with and avoids the twisting.

Each time you change a thread or start a new colour, always hold the new thread end at the back of the fabric with your finger. Don't knot the end though!

1 Separate your six stranded thread in to two stranded lengths. Thread onto your needle. Do not knot the end of the thread.

2 Start your first stitch by inserting your needle from the back of the fabric.

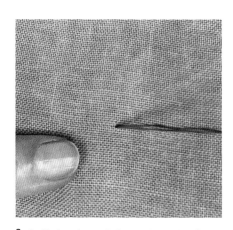

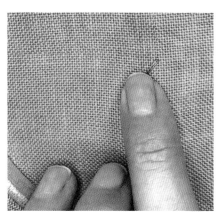

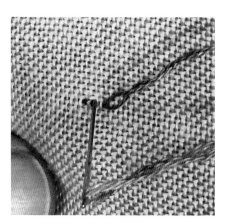

3 Pull the thread through to the front of the fabric.

4 Hold the other end of the thread against the back of the fabric with your finger. Work a couple of stitches before letting go of the thread end.

5 Continue to stitch, following the relevant chart or design. Pull the thread gently through the fabric to ensure it doesn't get tangled as you work.

FINISHING YOUR STITCHING

I recommend working with one colour thread at a time and then fastening off once finished. You can keep going with another length of the same coloured thread or start a new colour if you like, depending on the design you're working on. I advise against carrying threads across the back of your work as they may show through on the front of your stitching, especially if you're using dark colours (plus, it's a waste of thread!).

When you come to the end of a length of thread or need to change colours, you will want to finish your work neatly and ensure your precious stitching doesn't come loose.

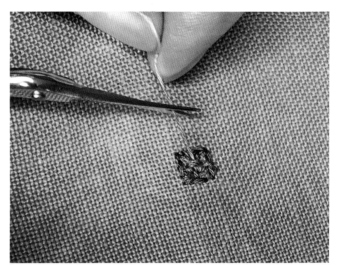

1 Pass your needle through several threads on the back of your work to secure your thread.

2 Cut the thread and, again, no knots!

ATTACHING A BACKING TO A FINISHED HOOP

These instructions are for a 21.5cm (8½in) embroidery hoop, but you can adjust the sizes of the various components for different size hoops.

1 Cut out three roughly circular shapes from wadding/batting, measuring 12cm (4¾in), 16cm (6¼in) and 21cm (8¼in) across, as shown on the left.

2 Cut a 21cm (8¼in) circle from cardboard.

3 Cut a 26cm (10¼in) circle from ivory cotton fabric.

4 Cut a long length of linen thread, around 1.6m (1¾yd), and fold in half.

5 Place the cardboard circle in the centre of the ivory cotton fabric circle.

6 Leave an 8cm (3¼in) long end of the linen thread and, using large tacking/basting stitches, sew around the fabric circle 1cm (⅜in) from the edge until you reach the other side (as shown on the left). Cut the thread, leaving an 8cm (3¼in) length of thread after the last stitch.

7 Pull tightly on each end of the thread and this will fold the edges of the ivory material neatly over the cardboard circle. Tie a knot to secure the material onto the cardboard backing circle.

8 Place the finished work in the centre of the hoop. Secure in place with the second part of the hoop.

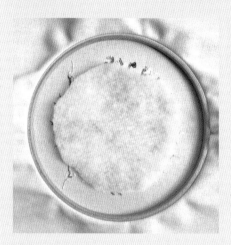

9 Place the 12cm (4¾in) wide circle of wadding/batting inside the back of the hoop, then place the 16cm (6¼in) wide circle on top, and finish with 21cm (8¼in) wide piece.

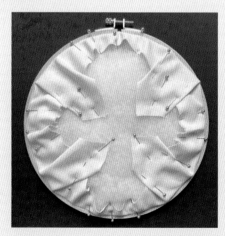

10 Fold the edges of the stitched fabric over the wadding/batting and pin to secure. If the folded fabric overlaps, trim away any excess.

11 Sew the folded fabric onto the wadding/batting.

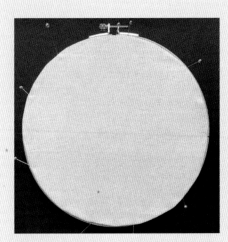

12 Now place the covered circle of cardboard from step 7 on the back of the hoop. Hold in place with pins.

13 Push the stitched front piece slightly out of the hoop. Use ivory cotton thread to sew the covered cardboard piece onto the back of the stitched piece. Sew all the way around the edge of the circle.

14 You may have to take the hoop off totally to be able to finish sewing on the backing, but you can easily put it back on once finished.

READING A BLACKWORK EMBROIDERY CHART

Blackwork is a form of counted embroidery, where each square on a chart represents a stitch – if you have ever done any cross stitch, you'll see that blackwork charts are very similar to cross stitch charts.

Locate the centre of the chart using the small black arrows on each of the four sides – you can see these on the chart opposite. You can draw lines with a ruler, or trace over the chart using your finger to find the centrepoint. Find the centre of your fabric by either folding it (see page 18) or by counting stitches. One square on a chart represents one block on aida fabric and two threads on evenweave or linen fabric. In other words, stitch over one block on aida for one stitch and over two threads on evenweave or linen for one stitch. One square/ count on aida fabric or one stitch/count (two threads) on evenweave or linen fabric is one square on the chart.

You should always start stitching from the centre of the piece of fabric you're working on. This is to make sure that your embroidery will fit, and to help keep your work smooth and even.

On the chart, each coloured line represents a thread colour according to the key. Coloured lines are to be stitched using backstitch; a solid coloured square on the chart represents a cross stitch worked in the colour represented on the key (see page 92 for an example). Some cross stitches also outlined with backstitch to make them stand out on the design. These are illustrated on the charts as a slightly larger coloured square (see for example the holly berries on the winter Tree of Life on pages 116–117). See the stitch guide on pages 16–17 for more on the stitches used.

An example of a blackwork embroidery chart. The key is shown to the right.

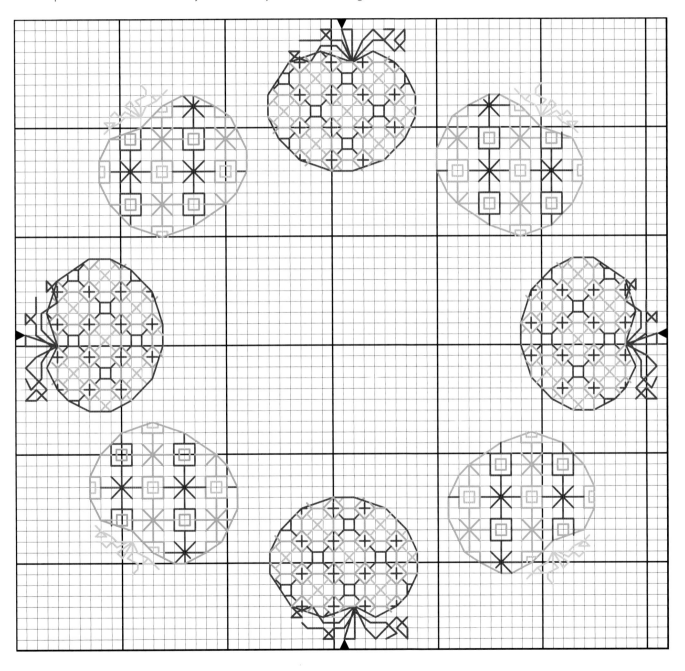

THE PROJECTS

TREE OF LIFE HOOP SPRING

I was inspired to design the spring Tree of Life after running two 'stitch-alongs', which had the Tree of Life as their theme. They were both cross stitch versions and, being a fan of these trees, I thought that it would be fun to use blackwork instead and have a Tree of Life to introduce each section of this book. This spring Tree of Life is buzzing with bees, budding new leaves and flowers, and pretty good-luck charm ladybirds.

MATERIALS

- 32-count evenweave: 30 x 30cm (12 x 12in)
  I used Zweigart murano in ivory (no. 32)
- Embroidery threads (see colour key, page 92)
- 21.5cm (8½in) wooden embroidery hoop
- Natural linen sewing thread
- Ivory cotton sewing thread
- Cotton wadding/batting, approx 50 x 50cm (20 x 20in)
- 2mm (¹⁄₁₆in) thick cardboard, approx 25 x 25cm (10 x 10in)
- Ivory cotton fabric, approx 30 x 30cm (12 x 12in)

TOOLS

- Blunt-ended tapestry needle
- Sharp-ended sewing needle

SIZES

- Finished size in stitches: 110 x 110
- Finished stitched piece: 18.5cm (7¼in)

STITCHING INSTRUCTIONS

1 Use the chart on pages 92–93. Find the centre of the chart using the arrows on each side and begin stitching from the centre of your fabric.

2 Stitch the tree trunk first and then work outwards to add the branches and roots. Once you have the bare tree stitched, it will be easier to sew the additional details.

3 When you have completed the stitching, iron the whole piece carefully on the reverse side.

ASSEMBLING INSTRUCTIONS

4 See pages 20–22 for how to attach a backing to your finished hoop.

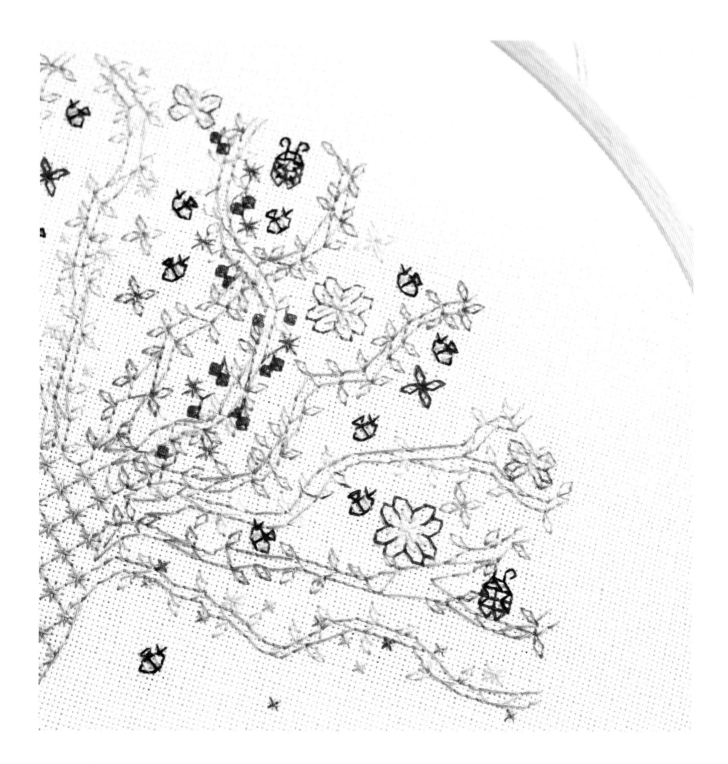

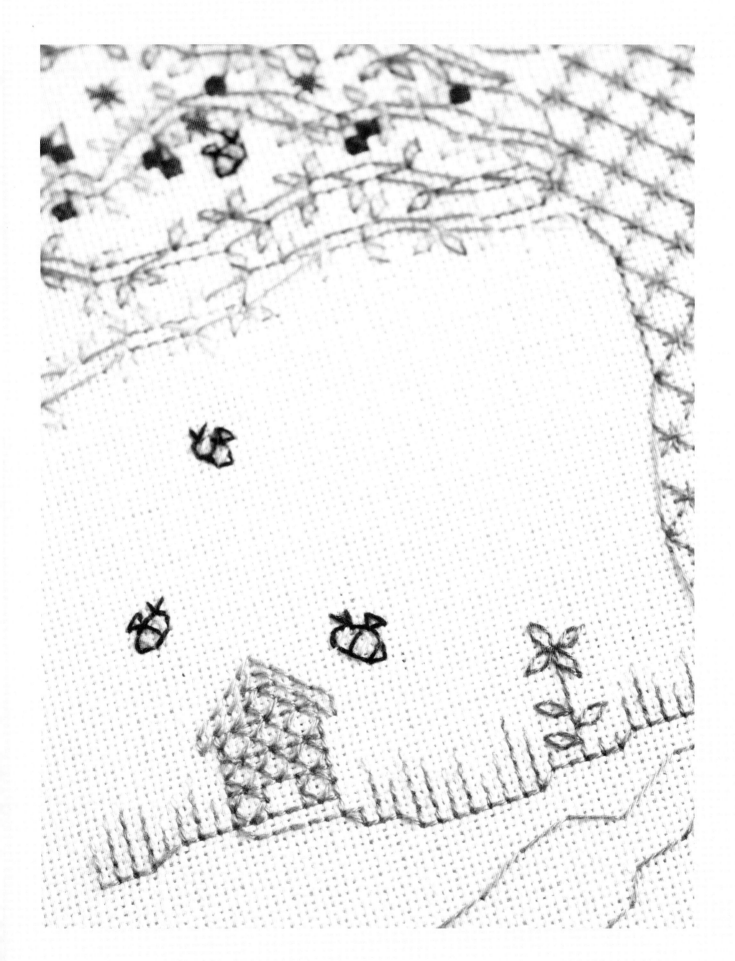

TULIP PINKEEP SPRING

I love designing and stitching pinkeeps and find them a really pretty
way to display my embroidery. This spring pinkeep is full of lovely
rainbow-coloured tulips and uses a lot of simple filler patterns
so you can practise your blackwork technique.
Each line of tulips uses two different shades of the same colour
(usually one light and one dark). The magic of these variegated hand-dyed
threads makes it look like there are many more shades used.

MATERIALS

- 32-count evenweave: 25 x 20cm (10 x 8in)
  I used Zweigart murano in sparkly white
- A piece of cotton material of your choice: 25 x 20cm (10 x 8in)
- Embroidery threads (see colour key, page 94)
- Two pieces of 2mm (1/16in) thick cardboard, each 20 x 15cm (8 x 6in)
- Two pieces of wadding/batting: two small rectangles, 10 x 7cm (4 x 2 ¾in)
- Two pieces of wadding/batting: two larger rectangles, 19 x 14cm (7 ½ x 5 ½in)
- Four different coloured organza ribbon, around 1m (1yd) of each
- Ivory cotton sewing thread

TOOLS

- Blunt-ended tapestry needle
- Sharp-ended sewing needle
- 22 white pearl-headed pins
- Double-sided sticky tape
- Masking tape

SIZE

- Finished size in stitches: 96 x 64
- Finished stitched piece: 16 x 11cm (6¼ x 4¼in)

STITCHING INSTRUCTIONS

1 Use the chart on pages 94–95. Find the centre of both the chart and your chosen fabric.

2 Start to embroider the design by stitching each tulip head individually. Fasten off the colour and then move on to the adjacent tulip. This helps you keep track of where you are on the chart and helps avoid making spacing errors.

3 Once you have stitched all of the tulip heads, go back and sew in the stems.

4 When you have completed your stitched design, iron it carefully on the reverse side.

ASSEMBLING INSTRUCTIONS

5 Measure your stitching, and add 2cm (¾in) extra to the measurement on each side to create the white border.

6 Cut two pieces of 2mm (⅟₁₆in) thick cardboard to the size measured in step 5.

7 Stick double-sided sticky tape around the outer edges of the cardboard on both sides.

8 Stick double-sided sticky tape in two parallel strips on the centre of each side of each piece of cardboard.

9 Stick the two small pieces of wadding/batting to the middle of each piece of cardboard.

10 Take the two larger rectangles of wadding/batting, and stick each one over the small rectangle of wadding/batting and stick them on the cardboard with double-sided sticky tape.

11 Centre your cotton material on one of the card pieces, over the wadding/batting. Pull the edges back and pin in place along the edges of the cardboard. Trim the fabric to 1.5cm (⅝in) from the edge. Adjust the tautness of the material by tightening or releasing the pins.

12 Stick the folded borders of material behind the card using the double-sided sticky tape that you placed there earlier.

13 Centre your finished stitched piece on the remaining piece of card, over the wadding/batting, and then pull the edges back and pin in place along the edges of the cardboard. Trim the fabric to 2cm (¾in) from the edge. Adjust the tautness of the material by tightening or releasing the pins.

14 Stick the folded borders of material behind the card using the double-sided sticky tape that you placed there earlier.

15 Stick a strip of masking tape along the edges of fabric on the back of the card.

16 Stick both finished cards together back to back.

The reverse of the pinkeep.

17 Using a needle and thread, fasten your pinkeep by sewing the two mounted cards together around the four edges.

18 Layer the four different coloured lengths of ribbon on top of one another. Pin together.

19 Wrap the layered ribbon around the edges to conceal the sewing, holding it in place by pushing pearl-headed pins into the edges at evenly spaced intervals.

20 Finish by tying the ribbon into a pretty bow at the top of the pinkeep.

BEE PENDIBULE SPRING

What I love about pendibules is how effective and smart they look, despite being really simple to make. My bee pendibule is a large heart-shaped ode to the glorious bumble bees that we see and hear in springtime.

MATERIALS

- 32-count linen: 25 x 25cm (10 x 10in)
I used Zweigart linen in natural (no. 53)
- Embroidery threads (see colour key, page 97)
- Cotton wadding/batting, one small bag
- Colour-coordinated organza ribbon, two lengths of 35cm (13¾in), in a colour of your choice
- Red cotton sewing thread

TOOLS

- Blunt-ended tapestry needle
- Sharp-ended sewing needle

SIZE

- Finished size in stitches: 126 x 126
- Finished stitched piece: 21 x 21cm (8¼ x 8¼in)

STITCHING INSTRUCTIONS

1 Use the chart on pages 96–97. Find and draw a mark on the centre by aligning the four arrows on the edges of the chart. From there, count the number of squares (diagonally here) that you need to get to the hive, and stitch that first.

2 Next, stitch the bees and flowers either side of the hive.

3 From the last flowers, count the squares to the upper row of flowers and stitch the top flowers, and then add the bees, ladybirds and so on until it is complete. (If you find it hard to count out from the centre point on the fabric, use a larger piece of fabric that will be big enough for the whole design, and start by stitching the hive, then count out from that.)

4 When you have completed the stitched piece, iron it carefully on the reverse side.

ASSEMBLING INSTRUCTIONS

5 Trim the square to 8mm (⅝in) from the edge of the backstitches and fold the edges under.

6 Fold the square pendibule along its diagonal, giving you a triangle.

7 Thread a pointed sewing needle with one long strand of red thread and tie a small knot at the end.

8 Pull the needle through the right-hand top corner of the triangle, from the inside out. The knot should stop the thread inside the triangle.

9 Whipstitch both edges together, passing through the two backstitches on both sides of your triangle, using the same method as for a biscornu (see page 40).

10 Continue down to the central tip and keep going. If you run out of thread use another knotted strand and come up from inside out, under some of the already whipstitched area.

11 Leave a small space, approx 3cm (1¼in), and stuff the pendibule with cotton filling. The pendibule should feel quite full – don't hesitate to fill it well!

12 Once you are satisfied with the firmness of the stuffing, close the remaining backstitches with the same techique.

13 Using a long-eyed needle, thread the two lengths of ribbon through each top corner.

14 Fold both corners upwards towards the top and tie two bows using the four pieces of ribbon: one bow above the pendibule and a second longer part with a knot, in order to hang it up.

FOB TRIO
SPRING

This collection of three accessories bring some extra colour to the spring section of this book. I've used some brightly coloured linens to stitch a coordinated biscornu, mini scissor cushion and humbug pincushion. The three designs are decorated with spring flowers and fluttery insects, such as dragonflies and butterflies.

BUTTERFLY BISCORNU

MATERIALS

- 32-count linen: 10 x 10cm (4 x 4in)
  Mine are hand-dyed in paon (turquoise) and feuille (lime green)
- Embroidery threads (see colour key, page 98)
- Small amount of cotton wadding/batting
- Colour-coordinated organza ribbon, two lengths of 35cm (13¾in), in a colour of your choice
- Two buttons, about 5mm (¼in) diameter
- Dark purple cotton sewing thread

TOOLS

- Blunt-ended tapestry needle
- Sharp-ended sewing needle

SIZE

- Finished size in stitches: 36 x 36
- Finished stitched piece: 6 x 6cm (2¼ x 2¼in)

FLOWER CUSHION

MATERIALS

- Two pieces of 32-count linen: 8 x 8cm (3¼ x 3¼in)
  Mine are hand-dyed in feuille (lime green) and violette (purple)
- Embroidery threads (see colour key, page 99)
- Small amount of cotton wadding/batting
- 40 turquoise 2mm (¹⁄₁₆in) beads
- Key ring (that can be threaded through the beads used)
- Dark teal cotton sewing thread

TOOLS

- Blunt-ended tapestry needle
- Sharp-ended sewing needle

SIZE

- Finished size in stitches: 30 x 30
- Finished stitched piece: 5 x 5cm (2 x 2in)

BUTTERFLY HUMBUG

MATERIALS

- 32-count linen: 25 x 25cm (10 x 10in)
  Mine is hand-dyed in violette (purple)
- Embroidery threads (see colour key, page 101)
- Small bag of cotton wadding/batting
- Colour-coordinated organza ribbon, 60cm (24in), in a colour of your choice
- Lime-green cotton sewing thread

TOOLS

- Blunt-ended tapestry needle
- Sharp-ended sewing needle

SIZE

- Finished size in stitches: 100 x 50
- Finished stitched piece: 16.5 x 8.5cm (6½ x 3⅜in)

STITCHING INSTRUCTIONS: BISCORNU

1 Use the chart on page 98. Find the centre and stitch the design of the front side of the biscornu onto the turquoise fabric.

2 Add the backstitched outline, as indicated on the chart, around the design. Backstitch the outline onto the lime-green fabric piece too.

ASSEMBLING INSTRUCTIONS: BISCORNU

3 Trim the fabric edges 5mm (¼in) from the backstitch outlines. Fold under the edges on both pieces of fabric. Iron in place.

4 Fold the embroidered fabric in half to find the centre point of one edge, and iron flat. Match a corner of the lime-green fabric to this point.

5 Thread your sewing needle with dark purple thread, then secure the thread at the corner of the lime-green fabric, on the wrong side. Bring the needle through to the right side at the corner of the backstitching.

6 Sew through the first pair of two backstitches without passing through the fabric itself. Use the whipstitch technique, see page 17.

7 Continue to whipstitch around the edges, leaving a small gap for the filling. Use a couple of extra stiches at the corners to reinforce the biscornu.

8 Stuff the biscornu with wadding/batting, making sure that your cushion is really full for it to look nice and tight.

9 Whipstitch through the last backstitches to close the gap. Work the thread in among the other stitches to hide the end.

10 Your biscornu is almost finished! All you need to do now is sew a button to the centre on either side and draw the two together to create a 'dimple' in the middle.

11 Start by securing the first button on one side and, without cutting your thread, sew through the centre of the biscornu and through the other button on the opposite side.

12 Stitch through the cushion several times, each time resewing the buttons in place and pulling your thread firmly so that the buttons form the deep indent on each side, as you can see from the picture on the left.

13 Add a ribbon – sew it onto a corner of the cushion.

STITCHING INSTRUCTIONS: FLOWER CUSHION

1 Stitch your flower cushion design onto the lime-green fabric following the chart on page 99. As always, start in the middle of the chart (find the centre by using the arrows on each side of the chart: see page 22 for more on this) and start stitching from the centre of your fabric.

2 Backstitch the outline square around the design as indicated on the chart.

3 Add the backstitched outline to the piece of purple fabric.

ASSEMBLING INSTRUCTIONS: FLOWER CUSHION

4 Trim the fabric edges 5mm (¼in) from the backstitch outlines. Fold under the edges on both pieces of fabric and iron flat.

5 Bring the two pieces of fabric wrong sides together, so two of the folded edges meet.

6 Thread your sewing needle with dark teal thread. Tie a knot in the end of the thread, then secure it on the wrong side of the fabric, at the right-hand side of the edges you've just brought together, and bring the needle to the right side of the fabric at the beginning of the backstitching.

7 Whipstitch through the first pair of two backstitches without passing through the fabric itself.

8 Thread a bead onto the needle and secure in place in the corner of the square.

9 Continue to whipstitch around the edges, adding a bead every two backstitches, but leaving a 2cm (¾in) gap for filling. Work a couple of extra stitches at the corners to reinforce them.

10 Stuff the cushion with wadding/batting, making sure that your cushion is full for it to look nice and tight.

11 Whipstitch through the last backstitches to close the gap, adding beads as before. Work the thread in among the other stitches to hide the end.

12 Work the key ring through one of the corner beads and attach the cushion to your favourite embroidery scissors.

STITCHING INSTRUCTIONS: BUTTERFLY HUMBUG

1 Find the centre of the chart on pages 100–101, and begin to stitch your design, working outwards from the centre, and following the chart.

2 Backstitch a rectangular outline around the design as indicated on the chart.

3 Iron the whole piece on the reverse side carefully.

ASSEMBLING INSTRUCTIONS: BUTTERFLY HUMBUG

4 Trim the rectangle 1cm (⅜in) from the backstitched outline and snip across the corners to reduce the amount of fabric to avoid bulkiness when they are turned out.

5 Fold the edges under and iron flat.

6 Thread your sewing needle with lime-green thread. Tie a knot in one end of the thread and secure it on the wrong side of one short edge. Fold the fabric in half so the two short edges meet and whipstitch them together, through the backstitching (see page 17).

7 Turn the fabric and whipstitch the adjacent two edges together – you should now have a rectangular pocket shape. Finish off your whipstitching.

8 Find the point on the top folded edge of the pocket that is opposite the beginning of the whipstitching. Bring these two points together, then pin along the folded edge – you should now have a triangular shape.

9 Whipstitch along the pinned edges, as before, leaving a gap for the filling.

10 Stuff the humbug with plenty of stuffing to create a firm and full shape, then whipstitch the gap closed.

11 Fold the ribbon in half widthways and sew to one corner of the humbug. Tie in a pretty bow to finish.

TREE OF LIFE HOOP SUMMER

This section of this book opens with the summer Tree of Life. I've used beach-inspired colours to invoke this, the warmest season of the year. You'll find some cheerful bunting, a sandcastle and bucket, the odd starfish and a fish or two in the branches of this tree.

MATERIALS

- 32-count evenweave: 30 x 30cm (12 x 12in)
  I used Zweigart murano in ivory (no. 32)
- Embroidery threads (see colour key, page 102)
- Wooden embroidery hoop, 21.5cm (8½in) diameter
- Natural linen sewing thread
- Ivory cotton sewing thread
- Cotton wadding/batting, approx 50 x 50cm (20 x 20in)
- 2mm (1⁄16in) thick cardboard, 25 x 25cm (10 x 10in)
- Ivory cotton material, 30 x 30cm (12 x 12in)

TOOLS

- Blunt-ended tapestry needle
- Sharp-ended sewing needle

SIZES

- Finished size in stitches: 110 x 110
- Finished stitched piece: 18.5cm (7¼in) diameter

STITCHING INSTRUCTIONS

1 Use the chart on pages 102–103 and find the centre of the design.

2 Stitch the tree trunk onto the centre of your fabric. Then work outwards to add the branches and roots.

3 When you have stitched the bare tree, begin to add the additional details and leaves one by one, working from the centre outwards. Fasten off neatly after each section has been sewn.

4 When you have stitched your Tree of Life, iron it carefully on the reverse side.

ASSEMBLING INSTRUCTIONS

5 See pages 20–22 for how to attach a backing to your finished hoop.

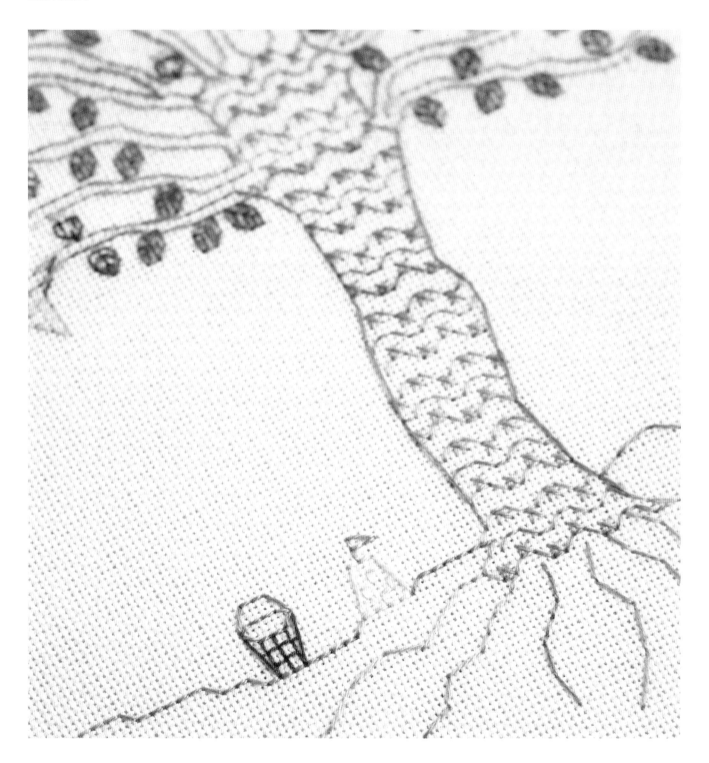

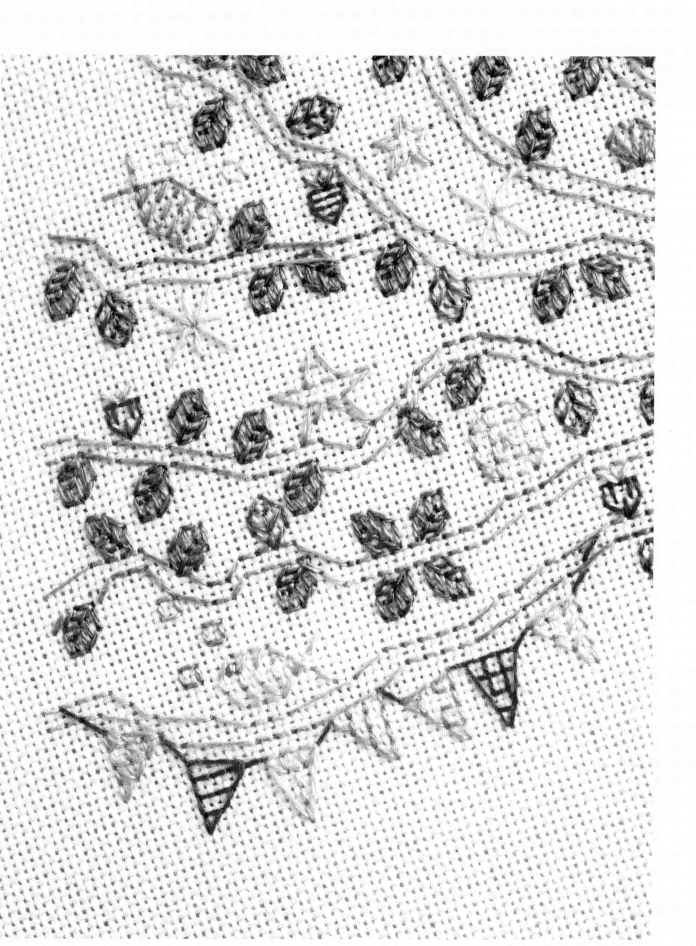

FLAMINGO TOTE BAG
SUMMER

This project brings together a modern blackwork flamingo design with a bright hand-dyed cotton tote bag. The colour shouts out summer and invokes the seaside, and looks amazing in contrast with the bright flamingo pinks.

MATERIALS

- 28-count sparkly evenweave: 25 x 25cm (10 x 10in)
  Mine is hand-dyed in lagon (light teal)
- Embroidery threads (see colour key, page 104)
- Pink cotton flanged piping cord, 65 x 5cm (25½ x 2in)
- Tote bag, 37 x 34cm (14½ x 13½in)

TOOLS

- Blunt-ended tapestry needle
- Sharp-ended sewing needle
- Sewing machine with zipper foot

SIZE

- Finished size in stitches: 67 x 42
- Finished stitched piece: 12 x 7.5cm (4¾ x 3in)

STITCHING INSTRUCTIONS

1 Stitch your flamingo design following the chart on pages 104–105. As always, start in the middle of the chart (find the centre by using the arrows on each side of the chart) and work outwards from the centre.

2 When the stitching is complete, iron the whole piece carefully on the reverse side.

ASSEMBLING INSTRUCTIONS

3 Trim the fabric to an oval shape, 24cm x 16cm (9½ x 6¼in), with the flamingos in the centre.

4 Pin the piping around the edge of the oval, making sure the edge of the piping flange matches the raw edge of the fabric.

5 Tack/baste the piping in place around the edge of the oval.

6 Snip into the seam between the piping and the fabric oval at 1cm (⅜in) intervals. This will help to make the machine stitching easier.

7 Now fold the piping outwards.

8 Pin the piped fabric oval onto your tote bag: mine is 9cm (3½in) from the top of the bag, 6cm (2¼in) from the base and 10cm (4in) from each edge.

9 Place a zipper foot on your sewing machine.

10 Place the bag on your machine so that you sew only through the front of the bag.

11 Machine stitch around the oval as close to the piping as possible.

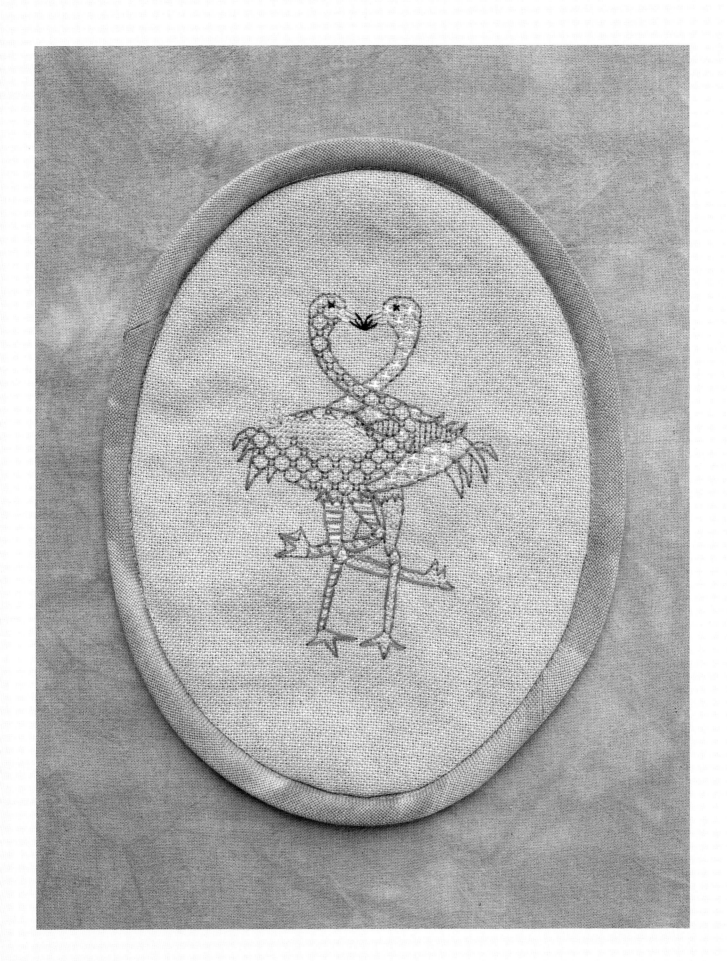

MARINE JEWELLERY
SUMMER

I really loved creating and stitching these mini nautical designs and making them into some summery jewellery. You can choose whether to wear it as a necklace or a brooch. The hand-dyed aida in saffron and blue shades really complement these quirky sea creatures.

MATERIALS

- 20-count aida: 10 x 10cm (4 x 4in) of each colour
  Mine are hand-dyed in safran (saffron), lagon (light teal), ciel (light blue) and paon (turquoise)
- Embroidery threads (see colour key, page 107)
- Four mini wooden embroidery hoops in the following sizes:
  vertical oval hoop: 6 x 3cm (2¼ x 1¼in)
  horizontal oval hoop: 6 x 3cm (2¼ x 1¼in)
  circular hoops: 5cm (2in) and 2.5cm (1in) diameter
- Cotton wadding/batting, 20 x 10cm (8 x 4in)
- Linen sewing thread
- Double-sided sticky tape
- Strong glue
- Brooch pin, 2cm (¾in)
- Chain, string or ribbon to make necklaces

TOOLS

- Blunt-ended tapestry needle
- Sewing needle
- Clamp or clothes pegs

SIZE

- Sizes in stitches:
  Seahorse: approx 35 x 17
  Tropical fish: approx 35 x 17
  Jellyfish: approx 25 x 25
  Starfish: approx 15 x 15
- Finished stitched pieces sizes: 6 x 3cm (2¼ x 1¼in),
  5cm (2in) diameter, 2.5cm (1in) diameter

STITCHING INSTRUCTIONS

1 Use the charts on pages 106–107 and find the centre of each design. Stitch your four marine designs on your fabric, working outwards from the centre and fastening off each colour neatly as you go.

2 Once you've stitched your designs, iron each one carefully on the reverse side before assembling them in their mini frames.

ASSEMBLING INSTRUCTIONS

3 Take each wooden mounting card from the mini hoops.

4 Cover one side with strips of double-sided sticky tape.

5 Place on the wadding/batting and cut around the wood.

6 Stick the piece of cut-out wadding/batting on one side of the wood backing using the double-sided sticky tape.

7 Cut a long piece of cotton thread. Fold in half.

8 Place each wooden mounting card on the back of each stitched piece, in the centre.

9 Leave a 4cm (1½in) end of the cotton thread, with no knot, and using large stitches, sew around each oval or circle about 1cm (⅜in) from the edge. Cut the thread 4cm (1½in) after the last stitch.

10 Pull tightly on the ends of the threads – this will fold the fabric edges neatly over the mounting cards. Tie a knot to secure.

11 Place the mounted pieces of stitching in the hoops, pushing them forward so that they show clearly.

12 Tighten the screw at the tops of the hoops to secure everything. Be careful not to overtighten as these parts of the hoops are fragile.

13 Put glue onto the edges of the hoops at the back, place the second wooden backing cards on top.

14 When you're happy with the placement, clamp or clip the hoop and backing together and leave over night to dry.

15 Thread a ribbon, string or chain through the tops of the hoops that you want to wear as necklaces. To wear one of the hoops as a brooch (such as the starfish design), glue a brooch pin onto the back.

55

MOBILE PHONE CASES
SUMMER

When I was thinking about what represented summer for me, I automatically thought of sunshine and of eating ice-cold lollies and delicious ice creams – the ones that melt quicker than you can eat them! These stitchable phone cases were the ideal shape for these yummy designs.

SUMMER TIME
MATERIALS

• Ivory stitchable phone case, to fit your phone (mine fits an iPhone 6+)
• Embroidery threads (see colour key, page 108)

TOOLS

• Sharp-ended embroidery needle

SIZE

• Finished size in stitches: 47 x 32
• Finished stitched piece: 13.5 x 5.5cm (5½ x 2⅛in)

ICE LOLLY
MATERIALS

• Black stitchable phone case, to fit your phone (mine fits an iPhone XS)
• Embroidery threads (see colour key, page 108)

TOOLS

• Sharp-ended embroidery needle

SIZE

• Finished size in stitches: 42 x 18
• Finished stitched piece: 11.5 x 5cm (4½ x 2in)

STITCHING INSTRUCTIONS

1 Stitch your chosen phone design following the charts provided on pages 108–109. As always, find the centre using the arrows on each side of the chart, and start stitching from the middle of your mobile phone case.

2 Stitch using a single thread and a sharp-ended embroidery needle as this will help you to be more precise when working through the holes in the plastic case.

3 Be sure to stitch over the ends of the thread, and weave the thread under the threads on the back when you finish each colour, to secure all ends in place.

4 Place your phone in the stitched case.

TREE OF LIFE HOOP
AUTUMN

Autumn is welcomed in this book with the autumn Tree of Life. I particularly love the autumnal season and the amazing colours that nature gives us at this time. There are plenty of colourful falling leaves, mature red grapes, ripe pumpkins and friendly spiky hedgehogs.

MATERIALS

- 32-count evenweave: 30 x 30cm (12 x 12in)
  I used Zweigart murano in ivory (no. 32)
- Embroidery threads (see colour key, page 110)
- Wooden embroidery hoop, 21.5cm (8½in) diameter
- Natural linen sewing thread
- Ivory cotton sewing thread
- Cotton wadding/batting, approx 50 x 50cm (20 x 20in)
- 2mm (1/16in) thick cardboard: 25 x 25cm (10 x 10in)
- Ivory cotton material: 30 x 30cm (12 x 12in)

TOOLS

Blunt-ended tapestry needle
Sharp-ended sewing needle

SIZE

- Finished size in stitches: 110 x 110
- Finished stitched piece: 18.5cm (7¼in) diameter

STITCHING INSTRUCTIONS

1 Stitch your Tree of Life design following the chart on pages 110–111. Start in the middle of the chart, stitching the tree trunk first, then add the branches and roots.

2 Once the bare tree is stitched, add the extra details and leaves, working in one colour at a time and fastening off each colour when finished.

3 Once your Tree of Life is fully stitched, carefully iron it on the reverse side.

ASSEMBLING INSTRUCTIONS

4 See pages 20–22 for how to attach a backing to your finished hoop.

PUMPKIN CITROLLI
AUTUMN

Autumn wouldn't be autumn without its pumpkins, and in this design you
have nine – eight stitched ones that make up one large pumpkin cushion!
I love this modern version of a pin cushion, with the pins on the edge
holding the delicate orange organza ribbon in place and thus leaving room
for the stitching to shine.

MATERIALS

◆ 32-count linen: two pieces, each measuring 20 x 20cm (8 x 8in)
I used Zweigart linen in natural (no. 53)
◆ Embroidery threads (see colour key, page 113)
◆ Beige cotton sewing thread
◆ Small bag of polyester wadding/batting
◆ Eight green pearl-headed pins
◆ Orange organza ribbon, 30cm (12in)
◆ Two buttons, the ones used here are 18mm wide (11/16in)

TOOLS

◆ Blunt-ended tapestry needle
◆ Sharp-ended sewing needle
◆ Compass and pencil

SIZE

◆ Finished size in stitches: 60 x 60
◆ Finished stitched piece: 10cm (4in) across

STITCHING INSTRUCTIONS

1 Use the chart on pages 112–113. Find and mark the centre by aligning the four arrows on the chart. From there, count the number of squares (horizontally or vertically) you need to get to one of the pumpkins, and stitch that one first.

2 Once your first pumpkin is finished, count your way to the following pumpkin on the chart and then on your fabric. Stitch the next pumpkin, then continue around the design, working in one colour thread and fastening off once finished.

3 Once the design is completely stitched, iron it carefully on the reverse side.

ASSEMBLING INSTRUCTIONS

4 Using a compass, draw two circles around your embroidery, on the reverse side, the first with a radius of 6cm (2¼in) and the second with a radius of 7cm (2¾in). You'll have two circles: 12cm (4¾in) and 14cm (5½in) in diameter.

5 Bring the two squares of linen together, with the stitched side facing inwards.

6 Using small, tight stitches, sew by hand around the smaller circle. Leave a 2cm (¾in) opening.

7 Trim by cutting around the larger circle, then snip into the seam edge at 1cm (⅜in) intervals.

8 Turn to the right side through the opening in the seam and stuff with wadding/batting. Using small, tight stitches, sew the opening closed.

9 Tie a knot in some thick yarn (I used 3 or 4 strands of the green thread used in the blackwork design).

10 Make a small stitch on the underside of the pin cushion, at the centre, then insert the needle in the centre of the pin cushion on the embroidered side and bring it out on the underside, where you began, to make a very large stitch going around the pin cushion. Pull on the thread so it makes an indent in the side of the pin cushion to begin creating the pumpkin shape.

11 Make another large stitch on the opposite side. Then make two more large stitches in the same way but in the other direction, so the pin cushion is quartered. Repeat to divide it into eight sections.

12 Sew a button to the centre of the top and bottom, stitching through the pin cushion.

13 Wrap a ribbon around the edge of the pin cushion to conceal the seam and secure with pearl pins.

HEDGEHOG PURSE
AUTUMN

I couldn't complete this section without designing a hedgehog. I love these little creatures and find them fascinating, and have stitched quite a few in my time as a designer. This one looks great on dark chocolate linen, surrounded by pretty autumn leaves on this sweet little clasp purse.

MATERIALS

- 32-count linen: 15 x 15cm (6 x 6in)
Mine is hand-dyed in chocolat noir (dark chocolate)
- Embroidery threads (see colour key, page 115)
- 8.5cm (3⅜in) curved clasp purse frame
- Dark brown strong cotton sewing thread
- Cotton wadding/batting: 20 x 20cm (8 x 8in)
- Cotton material for the lining
- Iron-on fabric adhesive

TOOLS

- Blunt-ended tapestry needle
- Sharp-ended sewing needle
- Scissors, paper and pencil
- Sewing machine

SIZE

- Finished size in stitches: 60 x 45
- Finished stitched piece: 10 x 7.5cm (4 x 3in)

STITCHING INSTRUCTIONS

1 Find the middle of the chart on pages 114–115, and start stitching from the centre of your chosen fabric.

2 For this design, use one colour thread at a time and work horizontally in rows to stitch all of the areas using that colour. Follow the chart and count the stitches to leave space for the other colours, carrying the thread across the back of your work (in this instance, the threads won't be seen from the front).

3 Fasten off each colour as you finish and continue to follow the chart, working with the next colour in the same way.

4 When you have completed your embroidery, iron it carefully on the reverse side.

13 Iron the two wadding/batting pieces onto the back of the stitched pieces using the iron-on fabric adhesive material shapes.

14 Place the two stitched wadding/batting pieces right side against right side. The wadding/batting should be on the outside.

15 Place the two lining pieces right sides together (the back of the lining material should be on the outside).

16 Place the paper template onto your stitched wadding/batting piece and mark where the hinges will be (A and B) with pins. Do the same for the lining piece.

ASSEMBLING INSTRUCTIONS

5 Create your own template by placing your purse frame onto a piece of paper and tracing around the top. Make sure to highlight where the hinges are located, marking them as A and B.

6 Draw the shape of the fabric part of the purse next - this is the size and shape you want the fabric section of your purse to be: draw half first, then fold the paper in half and trace over the first half to ensure that the template is identical on each side.

7 Draw a second outline around the first 1cm (⅜in) away from the original line. Mark the middle of the template at the top with a pen.

8 Cut out your template.

9 Using the template, cut out two identical shapes in the cotton lining material and two from the linen, one piece of which will have the hedgehog design on it.

10 Cut out two shapes in the wadding/batting material but slightly smaller: 5mm (¼in) less around the edge and 2cm (¾in) less along the top where the purse frame will be. This reduces the thickness and makes it easier for you to insert the purse into the frame.

11 Cut out two purse shapes from the iron-on fabric adhesive.

12 Mark the centre of the two stitching pieces of material and the two linings at the top with a contrasted coloured stitch, that you'll remove later. This helps keep everything aligned.

17 With your sewing machine, sew from A to B around the bottom of the stitched piece.

18 Do the same for the lining piece but leave a 4–5cm (1½–2in) gap at the bottom that you'll use to turn the layers right side out later.

19 Insert the lining pocket into the stitched wadding/batting piece. Pin in place.

20 With your sewing machine, sew along the top edges, between A and B, to join the stitched fabric to the lining.

21 Snip zig-zags into the seams to remove excess material and reduce overall thickness.

22 Turn the whole purse right sides out and hand sew the gap to close the lining.

23 Place the frame onto the purse, so it's centred on the top edge. Use tacking/basting stitches to hold the frame in place so it doesn't slip as you sew.

24 Using a double sewing thread, sew the material onto the clip with large stitches going from hole to hole.

25 Once the clasp is in place and the purse is finished, remove the tacking/basting stitches.

AUTUMNAL GRAPES
AUTUMN

Living in the south of France, vines, grapes and wine are an integral part of life here, especially in autumn when the *vendages* (grape harvests) take place. This colourful ring of juicy mature grapes is really complemented by the bright hand-dyed orange evenweave.

MATERIALS

- 32-count evenweave: 35 x 35cm (13¾ x 13¾in) *Mine is hand-dyed in safran (orange)*
- Embroidery threads (see colour key, page 117)
- Wooden embroidery hoop, 21cm (8¼in) diameter
- Natural linen sewing thread
- Ivory cotton sewing thread
- Cotton wadding/batting, approx 50 x 50cm (20 x 20in)
- 2mm (¹⁄₁₆in) thick cardboard, 25 x 25cm (10 x 10in)
- Ivory cotton backing material, 30 x 30cm (12 x 12in)

TOOLS

- Blunt-ended tapestry needle
- Sharp-ended sewing needle

SIZE

- Finished size in stitches: 120 x 120
- Finished stitched piece: 20cm (8in) diameter

STITCHING INSTRUCTIONS

1 Use the chart on pages 116–117 and find the centre. Begin to stitch the design following the chart, starting at the centre of your fabric.

2 Avoid carrying your threads across the back of your work, but instead fasten off each colour neatly before moving on to the next.

3 When your embroidered piece is complete, iron it carefully on the reverse side.

ASSEMBLING INSTRUCTIONS

4 See pages 20–22 for how to attach a backing to your finished hoop.

TREE OF LIFE HOOP
WINTER

The last season of this book is winter and is illustrated by the winter Tree of Life. I love the traditional colours of winter and this tree is full of holly, wrapped presents, bows, snowflakes and fairy lights on its bare branches.

MATERIALS

- 32-count evenweave: 30 x 30cm (12 x 12in)
  I used Zweigart murano in ivory (no. 32)
- Embroidery threads (see colour key, page 118)
- Wooden embroidery hoop, 21.5cm (8½in) diameter
- Natural linen sewing thread
- Ivory cotton sewing thread
- Cotton wadding/batting, approx 50 x 50cm (20 x 20in)
- 2mm (⅟₁₆in) thick cardboard, 25 x 25cm (10 x 10in)
- Ivory cotton material, 30 x 30cm (12 x 12in)

TOOLS

- Blunt-ended tapestry needle
- Sharp-ended sewing needle

SIZE

- Finished size in stitches: 110 x 110
- Finished stitched piece: 18.5cm (7¼in) diameter

STITCHING INSTRUCTIONS

1 Use the chart on pages 118–119. Find the centre of the chart and of your fabric.

2 Begin to stitch your Tree of Life design, starting with the tree trunk and working out to the branches and roots.

3 Once you have stitched the bare tree in brown, add the extra details and the holly and snowflakes in turn, neatly fastening off after stitching each item. Avoid carrying threads across the back of your work as they might show through the fabric on the front.

4 When your stitching is compete, iron the piece carefully on the reverse side.

ASSEMBLING INSTRUCTIONS

5 See pages 20–22 for how to attach a backing to your finished hoop.

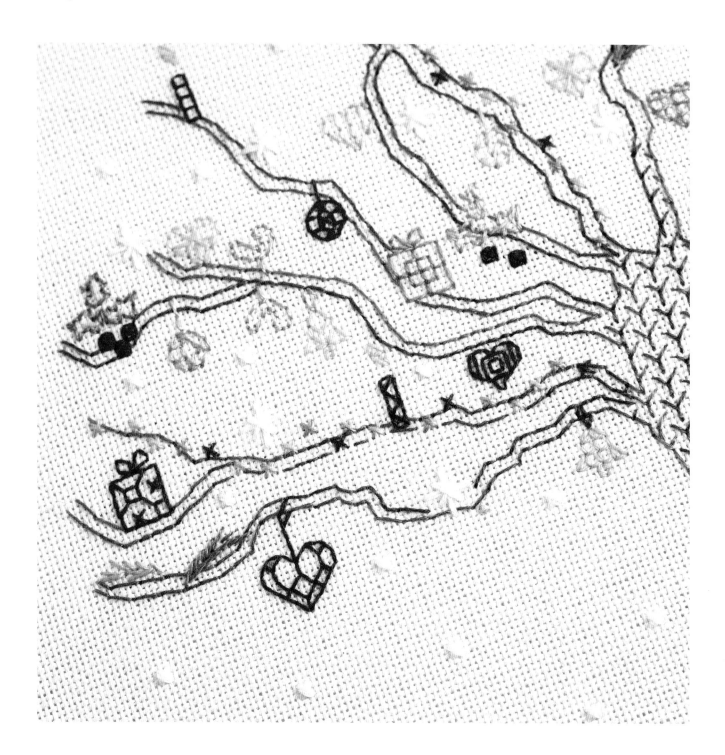

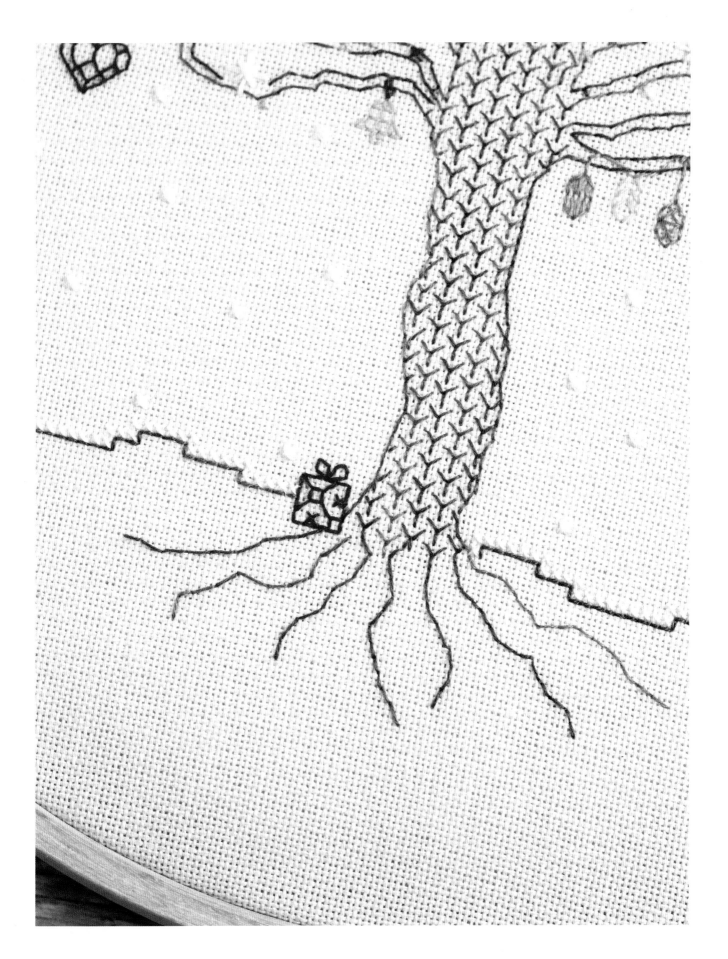

12 CHRISTMAS TREE DECORATIONS
WINTER

Winter, for me, is synonymous with Christmas and a beautifully decorated Christmas tree. I wanted to design some stars to hang on my tree and found that they looked great stitched with blackwork on these sparkly coloured linen squares. Red, green and white colours really evoke a traditional Christmas for me and I hope for you too.

MATERIALS

- 32-count sparkly linen: eight pieces of each colour (white, red and green), each measuring 10 x 10cm (4 x 4in)
  Mine are hand-dyed in white, noël (red) and sapin (fir green)

- Embroidery threads (see colour key, page 119)
- Red, green and white cotton sewing threads
- 5mm (¼in) wide white ribbon, 12 lengths of 20cm (8in)
- Cotton wadding/batting, 60 x 60cm (24 x 24in)
- Card, 1.4 x 1.4m (1½ x 1½yd)

TOOLS

- Blunt-ended tapestry needle
- Sharp-ended sewing needle

SIZE

- Finished size in stitches: 30 x 30 each decoration
- Each finished stitched piece: 5 x 5cm (2 x 2in)

STITCHING INSTRUCTIONS

1 Find the centre of each of your fabric squares, and use the charts on pages 120–121 to stitch each of your 12 Christmas tree decorations. Start stitching each design from the centre, and work outwards in the direction you prefer.

2 Sew the outside border on each square, as shown on the chart. The main decoration on each square is one colour, so no colour changes are required until you get to the border.

3 When your stitching is complete, iron each square carefully on the reverse side before you assemble them into hanging decorations.

ASSEMBLING INSTRUCTIONS

4 Cut 12 pieces of card, each measuring 5.5cm (2⅛in) square.

5 Cut 12 pieces from the cotton wadding/batting, each measuring 5cm (2in) square.

6 Stick strips of double-sided sticky tape on the front of squares of the card. Stick four pieces around each edge on the reverse.

7 Stick a cotton wadding/batting square on the front of each card square.

8 Centre each stitched star on a card on top of the wadding/batting. Trim the linen fabric 1.5cm (⅝in) from the edge. Fold the fabric edges to the back and stick them down behind the card using the double-sided sticky tape.

9 Cut 12 more pieces of card, each measuring 6cm (2¼in) square.

10 Stick strips of double-sided sticky tape on the front of the card squares. Stick four pieces around each edge on the reverse.

11 Centre each piece of plain linen on a card. Trim the linen fabric 2cm (¾in) from the edge.

12 Fold each corner of the fabric diagonally over the four corners of the card and stick down.

13 Fold back the edges towards the back and stick down using the double-sided sticky tape in place on the card. Make the corners as neat as you can. The covered side of these pieces of card will form the back of the decorations.

14 Fold the ribbons in half and sew one to the top left corner of each of the stitched squares to form the hanging loops.

15 Stick strips of double-sided sticky tape on the uncovered sides of the plain cards.

16 Stick the stitched squares on the appropriate contrasting plain squares: red star on white plain square; green star on red plain square; white star on green plain square.

17 Neaten the decorations by sewing the corners together with an invisible stitch.

FOLIAGE TRIO
WINTER

Winter is a beautiful time because of its shrubs and fir trees. This project was inspired by the Christmas carol 'The Holly and the Ivy'. This set of holly, ivy and mistletoe, stitched on icy coloured sparkly evenweave, come together to create a beautiful botanical winter trio.

MATERIALS

- 28-count sparkly evenweave: three pieces, each measuring 15 x 15cm (6 x 6in)
Mine are hand-dyed in white, ciel (light blue) and lagon (light teal)
- Embroidery threads (see colour key, page 122)
- Three decorative dishes/frames – the ones used here have a 12cm (4¾in) diameter inset
- Natural linen sewing thread
- Ivory cotton sewing thread
- Cotton wadding/batting, approx 50 x 50cm (20 x 20in)
- 2mm (⅟₁₆in) thick cardboard, 40 x 20cm (15¾ x 8in)
- Double-sided sticky tape

TOOLS

- Blunt-ended tapestry needle
- Sharp-ended sewing needle

SIZE

- Finished size in stitches: 62 x 45
- Each finished stitched piece: 11.5cm (4½in) diameter

STITCHING INSTRUCTIONS

1 Stitch the three designs following the charts on pages 122–125. As always, start in the middle of the chart (find the centre by using the arrows on each side of the chart) and stitch from the centre of your fabric outwards.

2 When the stitching is complete, iron each design carefully on the reverse sides.

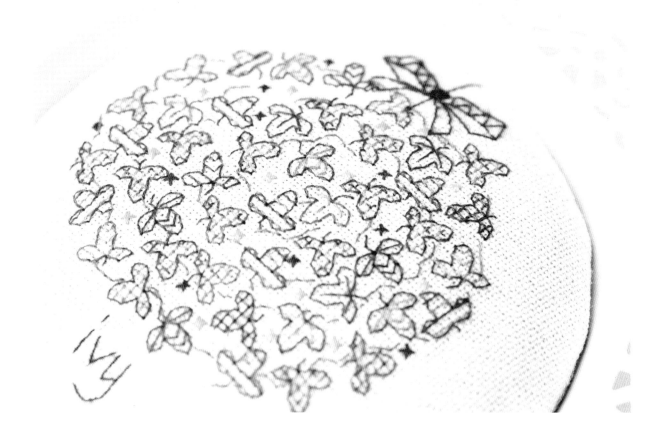

ASSEMBLING INSTRUCTIONS

3 Measure the finished design (as the finished size will depend on your choice of fabric).

4 Cut three circles of this size from the cardboard. Stick double-sided sticky tape on the front and around the edges of the back of the cardboard circles.

5 Cut three circles in the wadding/batting the same size as your finished stitched design.

6 Cut three circles in the wadding/batting 2cm (¾in) diameter smaller than the first.

7 Stick a smaller piece of wadding/batting onto each cardboard circle using double-sided sticky tape.

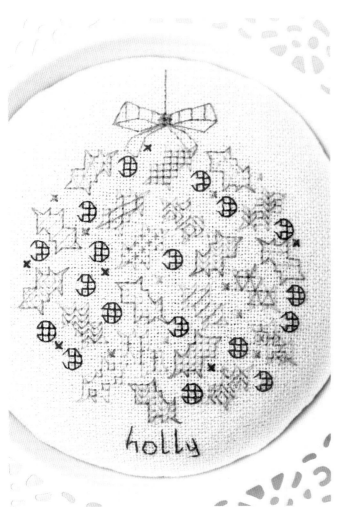

8 Stick the larger wadding/batting pieces over the top of the smaller ones.

9 Centre the stitched pieces on the wadding/batting-covered cardboard bases.

10 Fold the edges under, towards the back, and hold in place with pins, inserting them into the edge of the cardboard circles. You may need to snip the fabric edges to make them easier to fold under.

11 Adjust the placement of the pins and pull the fabric tighter if needed.

12 Once you're happy with the look of your stitched piece, stick the edges onto the back of your cardboard circle using the double-sided sticky tape.

13 Use glue or double-sided sticky tape to stick the covered card pieces into your three chosen dishes/frames. Leave to dry.

ROBIN CLOCK
WINTER

When I was little, I was a very proud young Brownie and I studied birds to get my birdwatching badge. I have loved watching birds ever since. The bird that used to light me up the most then was the robin, and it's still my favourite today. I have one that sits in the clementine tree outside my office window all winter long. I really wanted to include a robin design in this book and have added four to this winter clock.

MATERIALS

- 32-count linen: 30 x 30cm (12 x 12in)
Mine is hand-dyed in ciel (light blue)
- Embroidery threads (see colour key, page 127)
- Natural linen sewing thread
- Cotton wadding/batting, 25 x 25cm (10 x 10in)
- Circular clock face and mechanism, 22cm (8¾in) diameter
- Double-sided sticky tape
- Masking tape

TOOLS

- Blunt-ended tapestry needle
- Sharp-ended sewing needle

SIZE

- Finished size in stitches: 132 x 132
- Finished stitched piece: 22cm (8¾in) diameter

STITCHING INSTRUCTIONS

1 Use the chart on pages 126–127.

2 Start by stitching the central holly wreath first, working in one colour thread at a time, and fastening off after stitching each little shape. Avoid carrying red thread behind your white fabric as it may show through on the front.

3 After stitching the holly and berries in the centre, count the number of squares horizontally or vertically that you need to get to one of the robins and stitch that one first.

4 Once the first robin is finished, count your way to one of the adjacent numbers on your chart, and start stitching at the corresponding place on your fabric.

5 Continue stitching the other numbers, holly and robins.

6 When the stitching is complete, iron the piece carefully on the reverse side.

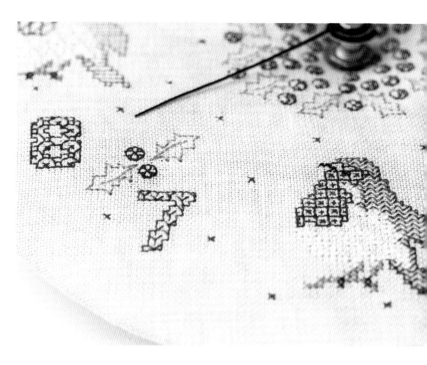

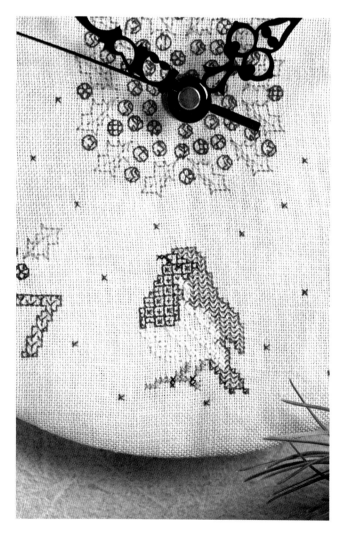

ASSEMBLING INSTRUCTIONS

7 Stick a thin piece of wadding/batting onto the clock face using double-sided sticky tape. Place the stitched piece face down on a clean and dry surface and place the clock face wadding/batting side down on top, centred on the design.

8 Trim the linen into a circle leaving a 4cm (1½in) margin around the edge of the clock face. Thread a sewing needle with a long piece of linen thread.

9 Leaving 8cm (3¼in) of thread at the beginning, sew around the circle, 1cm (⅜in) from the edge, using large stitches. Cut the thread 8cm (3¼in) after the last stitch.

10 Pull tightly on each end of the thread and this will fold the edges of the linen neatly over the clock circle. Tie a knot to secure.

11 Use masking tape to secure the fabric edges to the back of the clock.

12 Poke a needle through the hole in the clock face from the back through to the front. Use the needle to help separate the fabric fibres and make a hole big enough for the clock mechanism.

13 Insert the clock mechanism through the holes at the back and in the fabric. Fix the hands onto the front of the clock.

14 Place a battery in the mechanism and set the correct time on the clock!

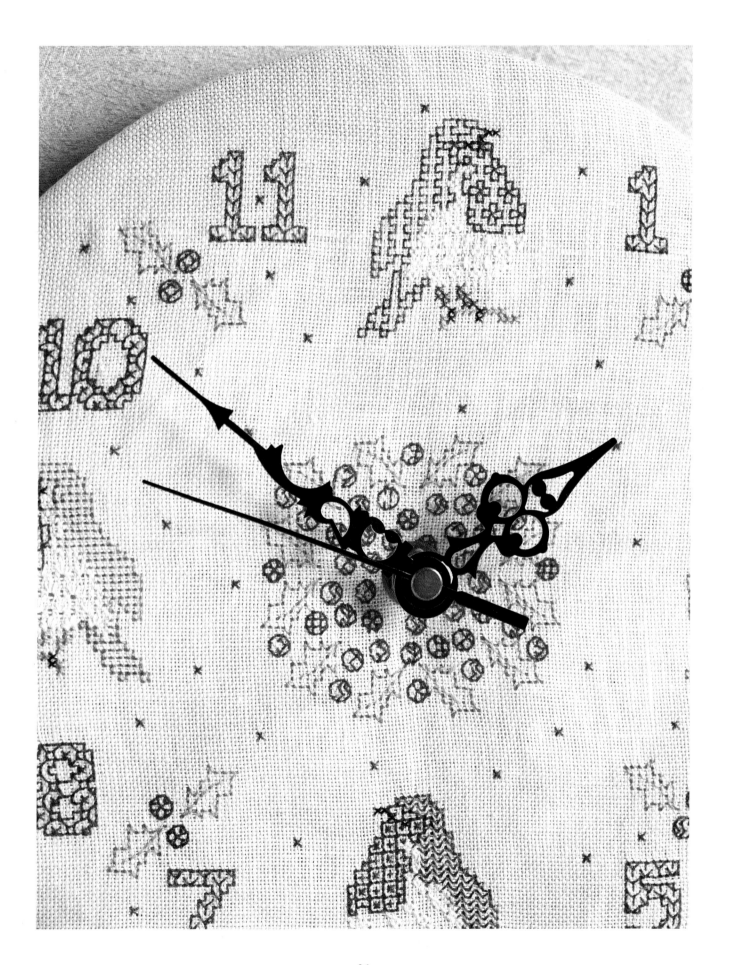

THE CHARTS
SPRING

These charts are also available to download free from the Bookmarked Hub: www.bookmarkedhub.com. Search for this book by title or ISBN: the files can be found under 'Book Extras'. Membership of the Bookmarked online community is free.

Tree of Life hoop, see page 26

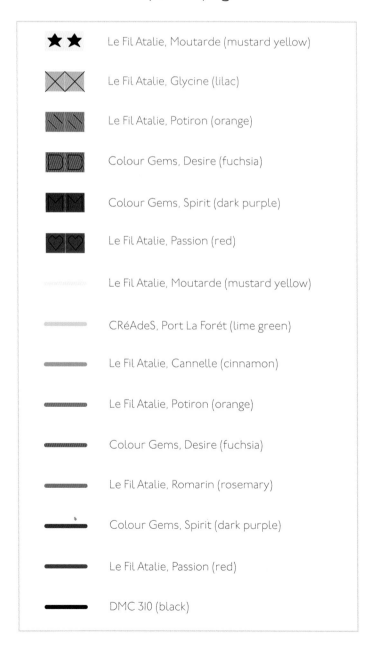

★ ★	Le Fil Atalie, Moutarde (mustard yellow)
⧖ ⧖	Le Fil Atalie, Glycine (lilac)
⧅ ⧅	Le Fil Atalie, Potiron (orange)
◨ ◨	Colour Gems, Desire (fuchsia)
◼ ◼	Colour Gems, Spirit (dark purple)
♡ ♡	Le Fil Atalie, Passion (red)
⋯⋯⋯	Le Fil Atalie, Moutarde (mustard yellow)
▬▬▬	CRéAdeS, Port La Forét (lime green)
▬▬▬	Le Fil Atalie, Cannelle (cinnamon)
▬▬▬	Le Fil Atalie, Potiron (orange)
▬▬▬	Colour Gems, Desire (fuchsia)
▬▬▬	Le Fil Atalie, Romarin (rosemary)
▬▬▬	Colour Gems, Spirit (dark purple)
▬▬▬	Le Fil Atalie, Passion (red)
▬▬▬	DMC 310 (black)

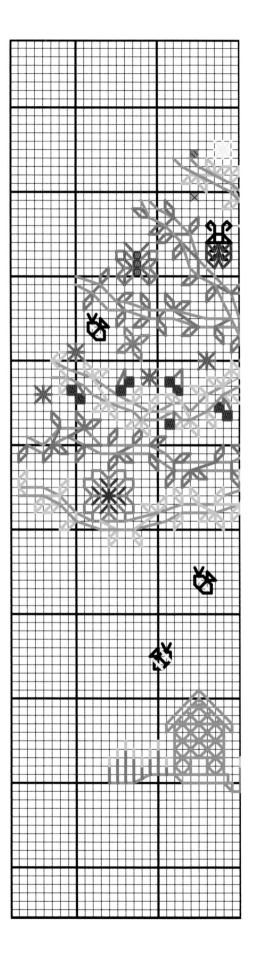

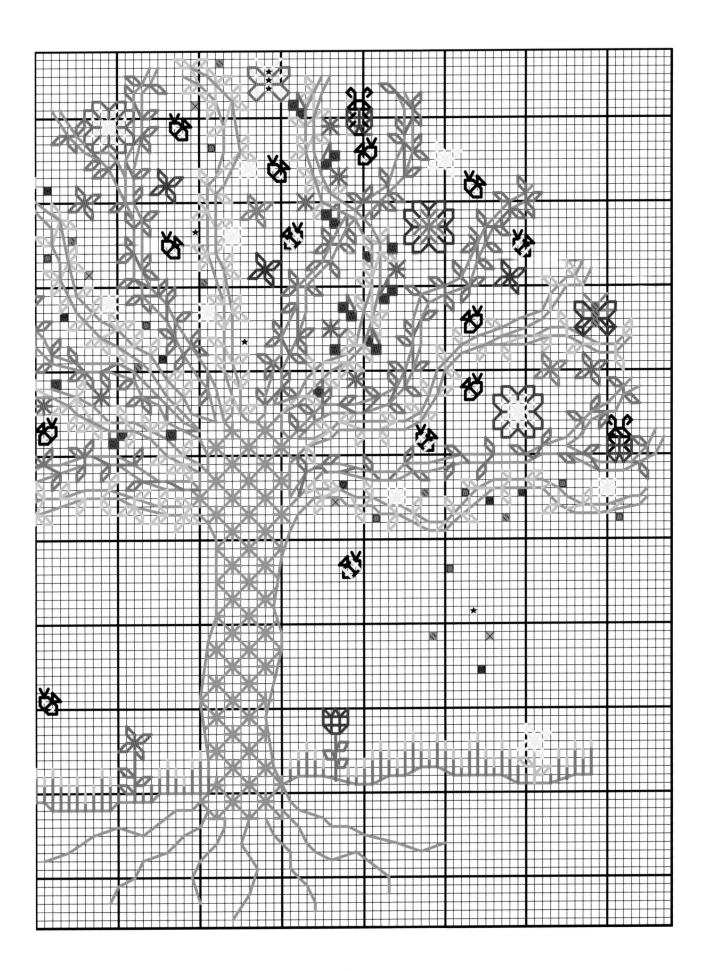

Tulip pinkeep, see page 30

66 CRéAdeS, Lorient (bright yellow)

Le Fil Atalie, Myrtille (mauve)

CRéAdeS, Lorient (bright yellow)

Le Fil Atalie, Opale (turquoise)

Le Fil Atalie, Moutarde (mustard yellow)

Le Fil Atalie, Myrtille (mauve)

Le Fil Atalie, Ortie (leaf green)

CRéAdeS, Pont L'Abbé (bright orange)

CRéAdeS, Le Palais (turquoise blue)

CRéAdeS, Port La Forét (lime green)

Le Fil Atalie, Potiron (orange)

Le Fil Atalie, Sapin (fir green)

Le Fil Atalie, Romarin (rosemary)

Colour Gems, Spirit (dark purple)

Le Fil Atalie -Passion (red)

CRéAdeS, Atlantique 4 (navy blue)

Le Fil Atalie, Gorgone (burgundy)

Le Fil Atalie, Encre (dark blue)

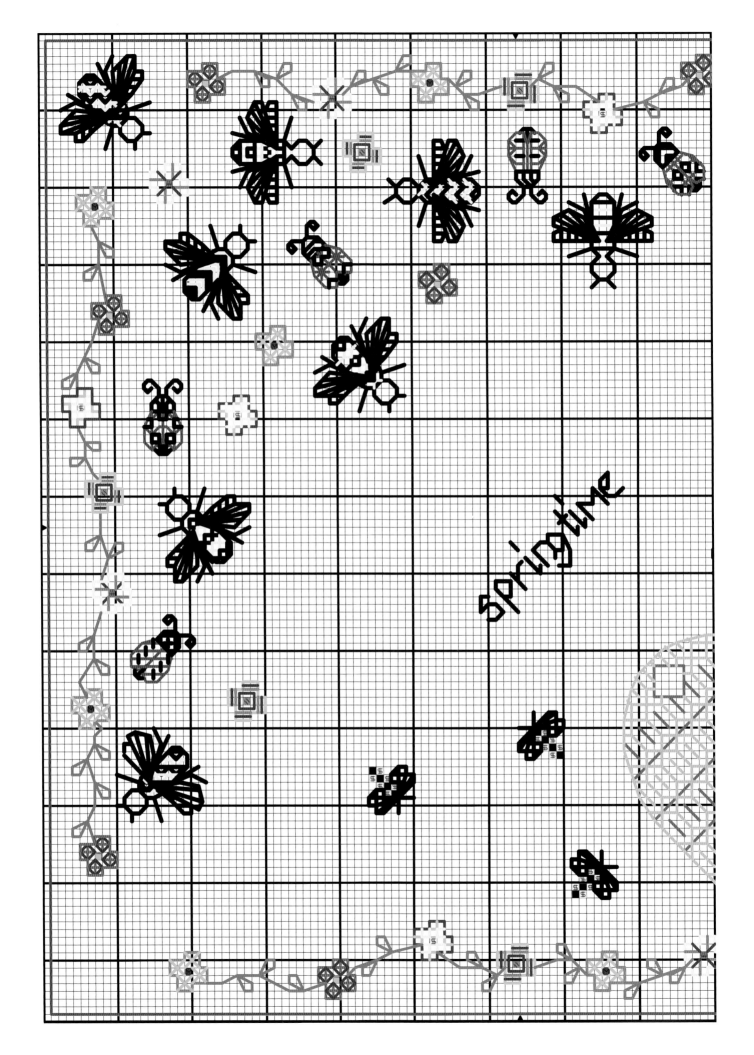

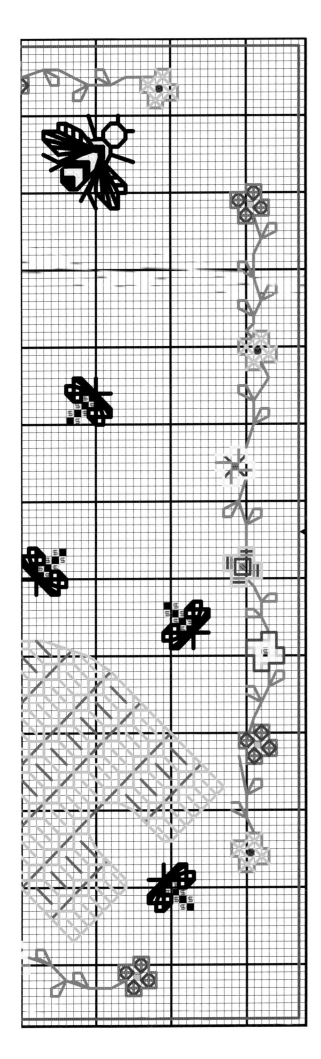

Bee pendibule, see page 34

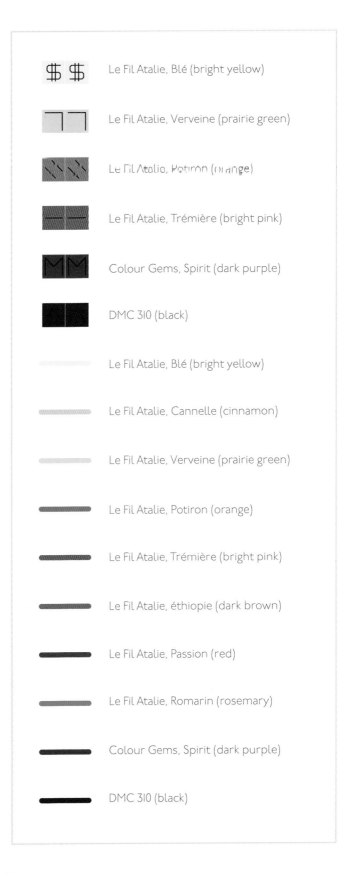

$ $	Le Fil Atalie, Blé (bright yellow)
	Le Fil Atalie, Verveine (prairie green)
	Le Fil Atalie, Potiron (orange)
	Le Fil Atalie, Trémière (bright pink)
M M	Colour Gems, Spirit (dark purple)
	DMC 310 (black)
	Le Fil Atalie, Blé (bright yellow)
	Le Fil Atalie, Cannelle (cinnamon)
	Le Fil Atalie, Verveine (prairie green)
	Le Fil Atalie, Potiron (orange)
	Le Fil Atalie, Trémière (bright pink)
	Le Fil Atalie, éthiopie (dark brown)
	Le Fil Atalie, Passion (red)
	Le Fil Atalie, Romarin (rosemary)
	Colour Gems, Spirit (dark purple)
	DMC 310 (black)

Fob trio, see page 38
Butterfly biscornu

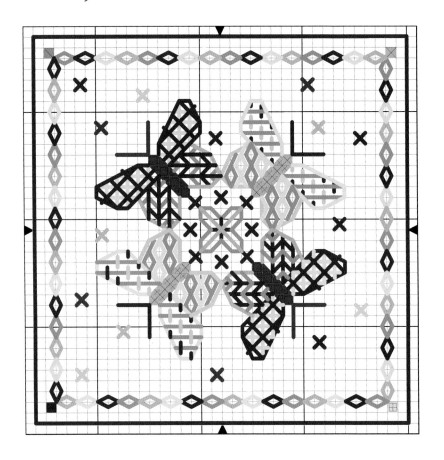

▦▦ Le Fil Atalie, Pistache (medium teal)	▬▬▬ Le Fil Atalie, Pistache (medium teal)
✕✕ Le Fil Atalie, Glycine (lilac)	▬▬▬ Le Fil Atalie, Glycine (lilac)
◨◨ Le Fil Atalie, Sauge (lagoon)	▬▬▬ Le Fil Atalie, Ortie (leaf green)
▮▮ Colour Gems, Spirit (dark purple)	▬▬▬ Le Fil Atalie, Sauge (lagoon)
▣▣ Colour Gems, Pétrole (very dark teal)	▬▬▬ Colour Gems, Spirit (dark purple)
	▬▬▬ Colour Gems, Pétrole (very dark teal)

Flower cushion

Le Fil Atalie, Lagon (light teal)

Le Fil Atalie, Trémière (bright pink)

Le Fil Atalie, Cassisine (berries)

Le Fil Atalie, Sauge (lagoon)

Colour Gems, Spirit (dark purple)

Colour Gems, Pétrole (very dark teal)

Le Fil Atalie, Lagon (light teal)

Le Fil Atalie, Trémière (bright pink)

Le Fil Atalie, Cassisine (berries)

Le Fil Atalie, Sauge (lagoon)

Colour Gems, Spirit (dark purple)

Colour Gems, Pétrole (very dark teal)

Le Fil Atalie, Lilas (light lilac)

Fob trio, see page 38

Butterfly humbug

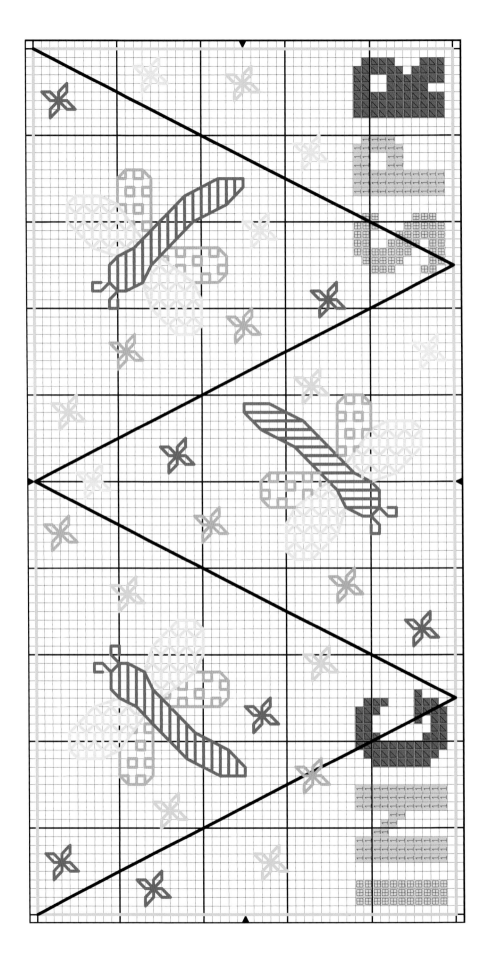

⊞⊞	Le Fil Atalie, Pistache (medium teal)
◪◪	Colour Gems, Calm (sea green)
1 1	CRéAdeS, Port La Forét (lime green)
▬	Le Fil Atalie, Pistache (medium teal)
▬	Colour Gems, Calm (sea green)
▬	CRéAdeS, Port La Forét (lime green)
▬	Le Fil Atalie, Lilas (light lilac)

Note
The black lines on the chart are to help visualize the edges of the humbug when it is assembled. These are not to be stitched, there are no black stitches on this project.

SUMMER

Tree of Life hoop, see page 44

 Le Fil Atalie, Écorce (light bark)

Le Fil Atalie, Blé (bright yellow)

Le Fil Atalie, Cognac (golden yellow)

Le Fil Atalie, Brique (light coral)

Le Fil Atalie, Verveine (prairie green)

Le Fil Atalie, Framboise (raspberry)

Le Fil Atalie, Géranium (dark coral)

Le Fil Atalie, Écorce (light bark)

Le Fil Atalie, Potiron (orange)

Le Fil Atalie, Trémière (bright pink)

Le Fil Atalie, Baobab (camouflage green)

Le Fil Atalie, Pacifique (bright blue)

Le Fil Atalie, Passion (red)

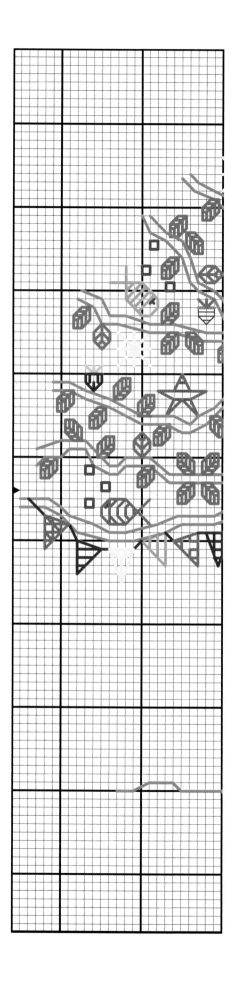

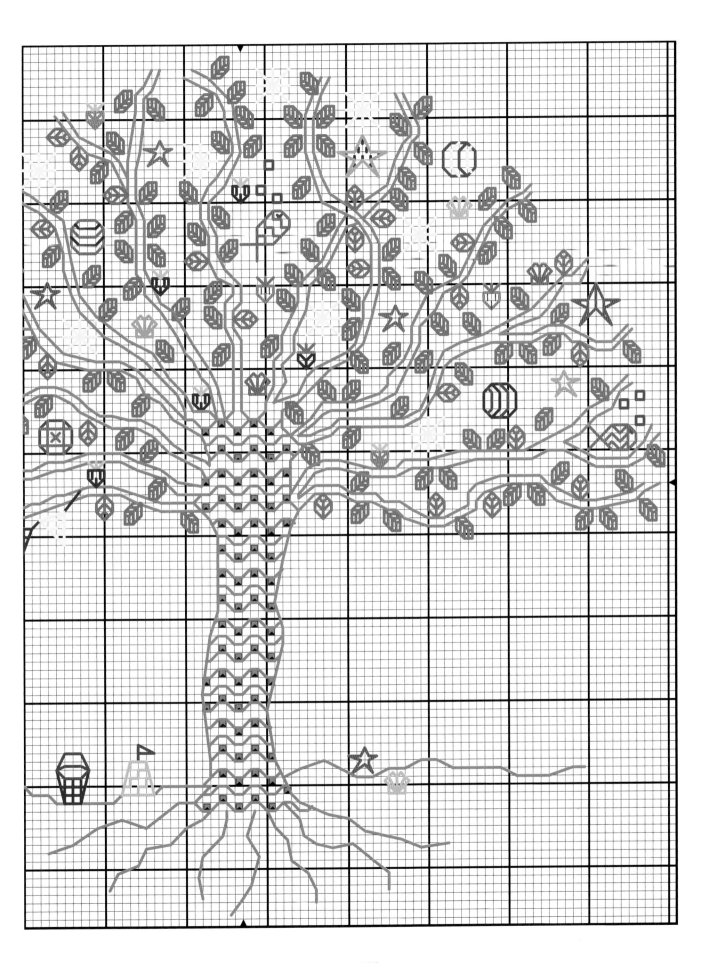

Flamingo tote bag, see page 48

Colour Gems, Youth (light pink)

Le Fil Atalie, Onyx (grey/black)

Colour Gems, Youth (light pink)

Le Fil Atalie, Géranium (dark coral)

Le Fil Atalie, Lagon (light teal)

Colour Gems, Desire (fuchsia)

Colour Gems, Calm (sea green)

Le Fil Atalie, Onyx (grey/black)

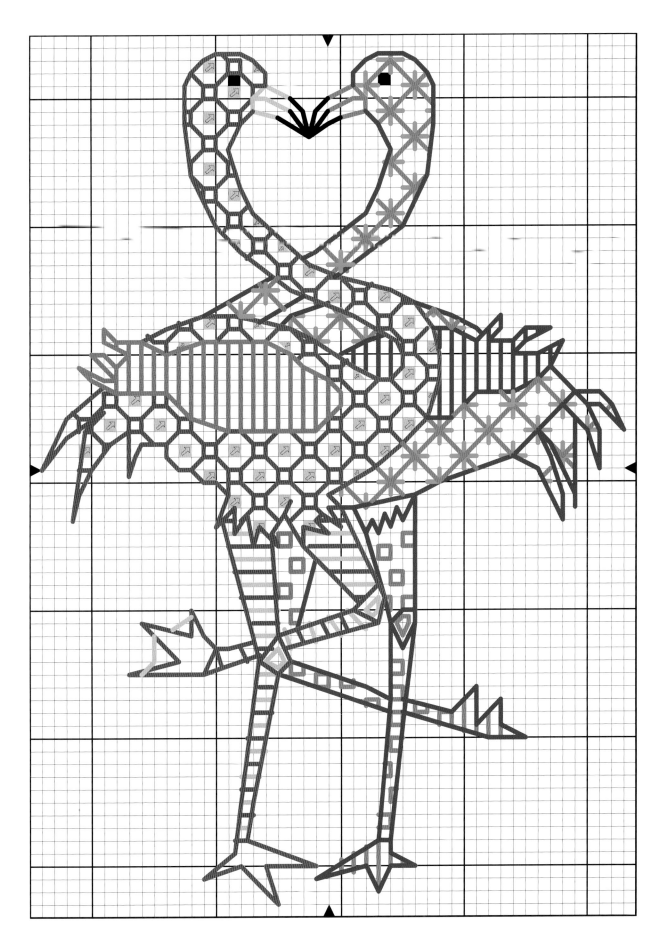

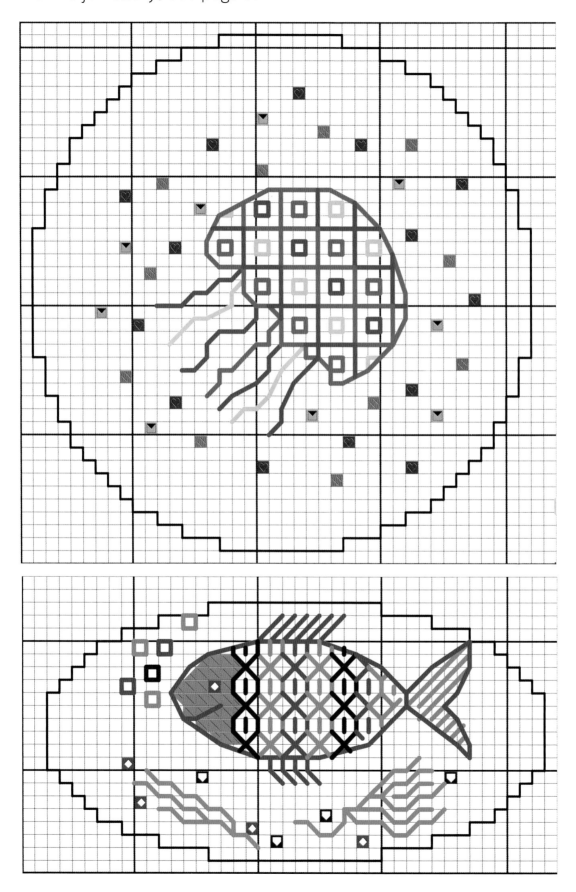

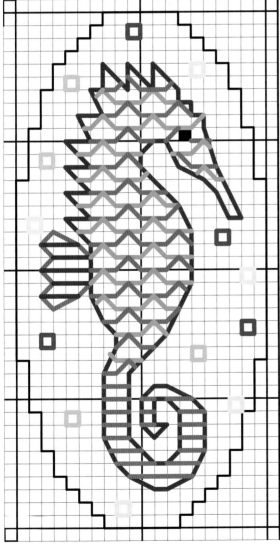

	Le Fil Atalie, Potiron (orange)	
	Le Fil Atalie, Géranium (dark coral)	
	Le Fil Atalie, Sauge (lagoon)	
	Le Fil Atalie, Sapin (fir green)	
	Le Fil Atalie, Passion (red)	
	Le Fil Atalie, Pacifique (bright blue)	
	Le Fil Atalie, Encre (dark blue)	
	Le Fil Atalie, Onyx (grey/black)	
	Le Fil Atalie, Lagon (light teal)	
	Colour Gems, Flow (bright turquoise)	
	Le Fil Atalie, Potiron (orange)	
	Le Fil Atalie, Géranium (dark coral)	
	Le Fil Atalie, Sauge (lagoon)	
	Le Fil Atalie, Piment (chilli red)	
	Le Fil Atalie, Pacifique (bright blue)	
	Le Fil Atalie, Encre (dark blue)	

Note
The black outlines on these charts are to help visualize the shape of the jewellery pieces. These are not to be stitched.

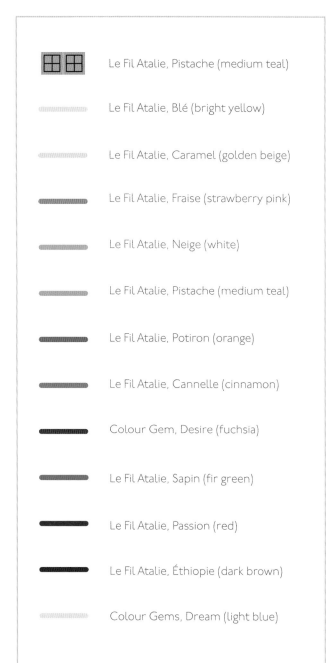

Le Fil Atalie, Pistache (medium teal)

Le Fil Atalie, Blé (bright yellow)

Le Fil Atalie, Caramel (golden beige)

Le Fil Atalie, Fraise (strawberry pink)

Le Fil Atalie, Neige (white)

Le Fil Atalie, Pistache (medium teal)

Le Fil Atalie, Potiron (orange)

Le Fil Atalie, Cannelle (cinnamon)

Colour Gem, Desire (fuchsia)

Le Fil Atalie, Sapin (fir green)

Le Fil Atalie, Passion (red)

Le Fil Atalie, Éthiopie (dark brown)

Colour Gems, Dream (light blue)

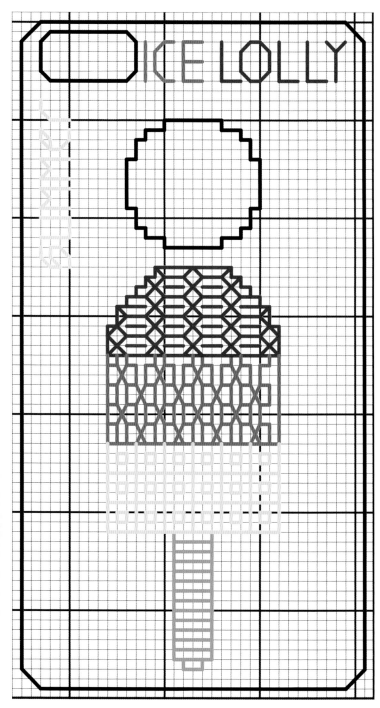

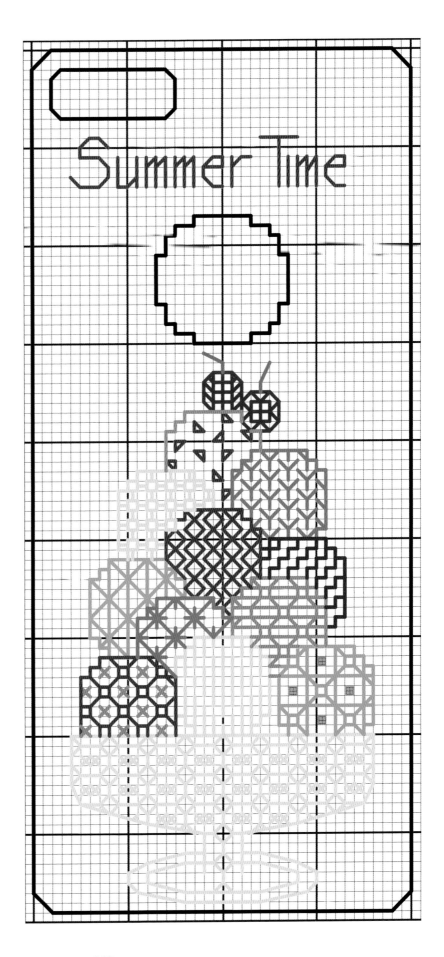

AUTUMN

Tree of Life hoop, see page 60

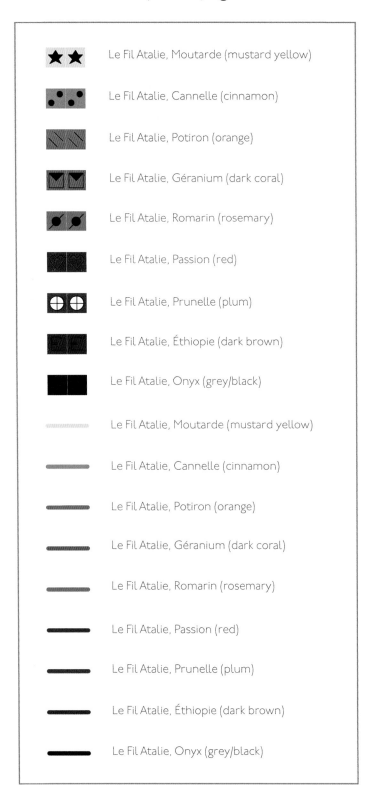

★ ★ Le Fil Atalie, Moutarde (mustard yellow)

Le Fil Atalie, Cannelle (cinnamon)

Le Fil Atalie, Potiron (orange)

Le Fil Atalie, Géranium (dark coral)

Le Fil Atalie, Romarin (rosemary)

Le Fil Atalie, Passion (red)

Le Fil Atalie, Prunelle (plum)

Le Fil Atalie, Éthiopie (dark brown)

Le Fil Atalie, Onyx (grey/black)

Le Fil Atalie, Moutarde (mustard yellow)

Le Fil Atalie, Cannelle (cinnamon)

Le Fil Atalie, Potiron (orange)

Le Fil Atalie, Géranium (dark coral)

Le Fil Atalie, Romarin (rosemary)

Le Fil Atalie, Passion (red)

Le Fil Atalie, Prunelle (plum)

Le Fil Atalie, Éthiopie (dark brown)

Le Fil Atalie, Onyx (grey/black)

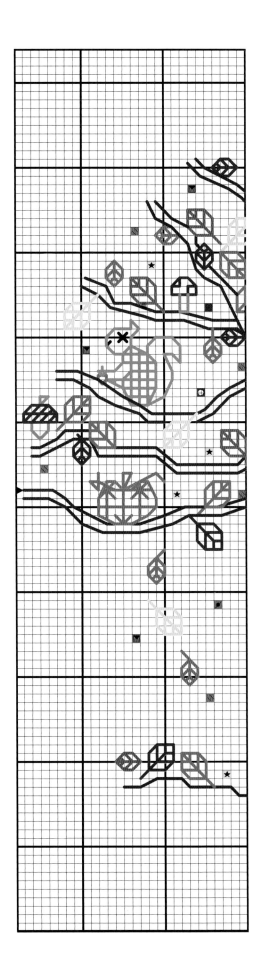

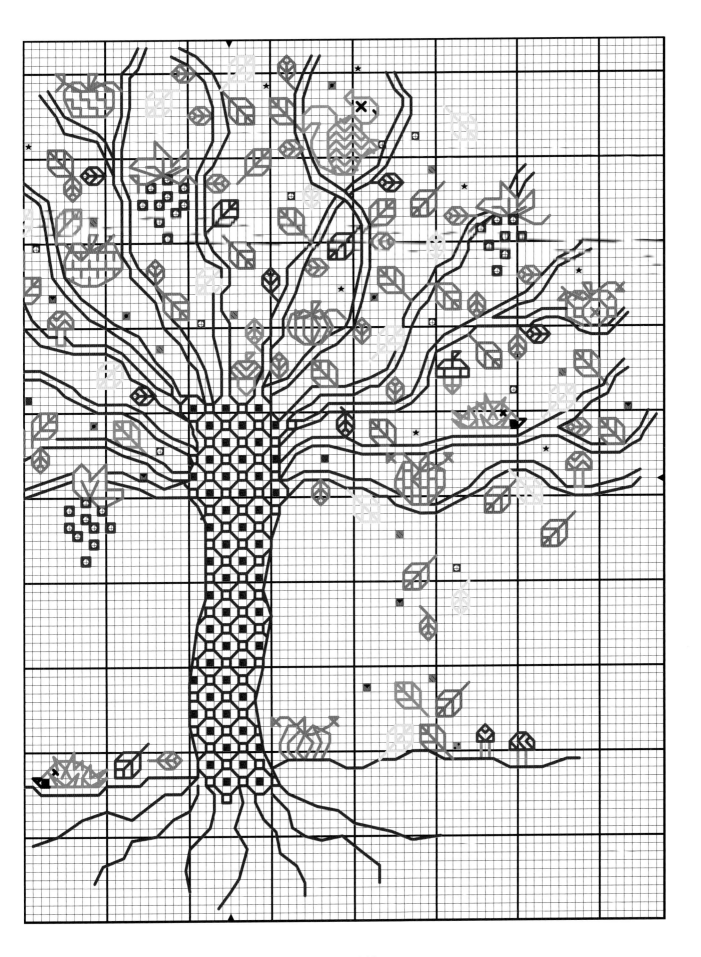

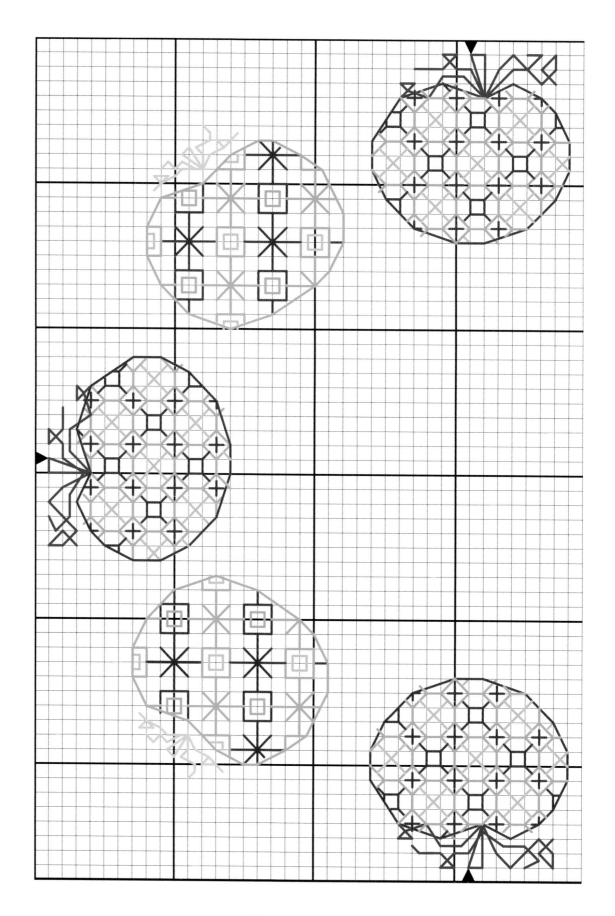

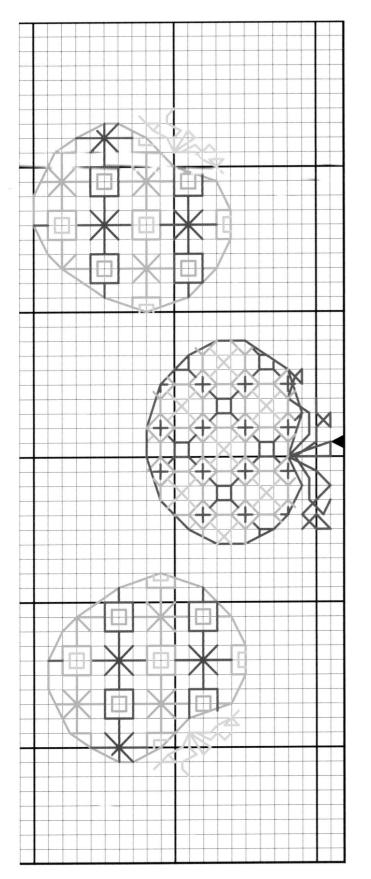

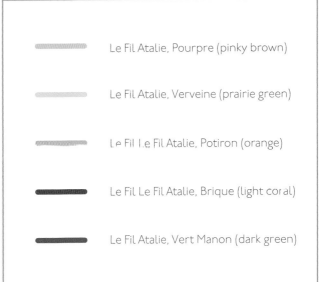

Le Fil Atalie, Pourpre (pinky brown)

Le Fil Atalie, Verveine (prairie green)

Le Fil Le Fil Atalie, Potiron (orange)

Le Fil Le Fil Atalie, Brique (light coral)

Le Fil Atalie, Vert Manon (dark green)

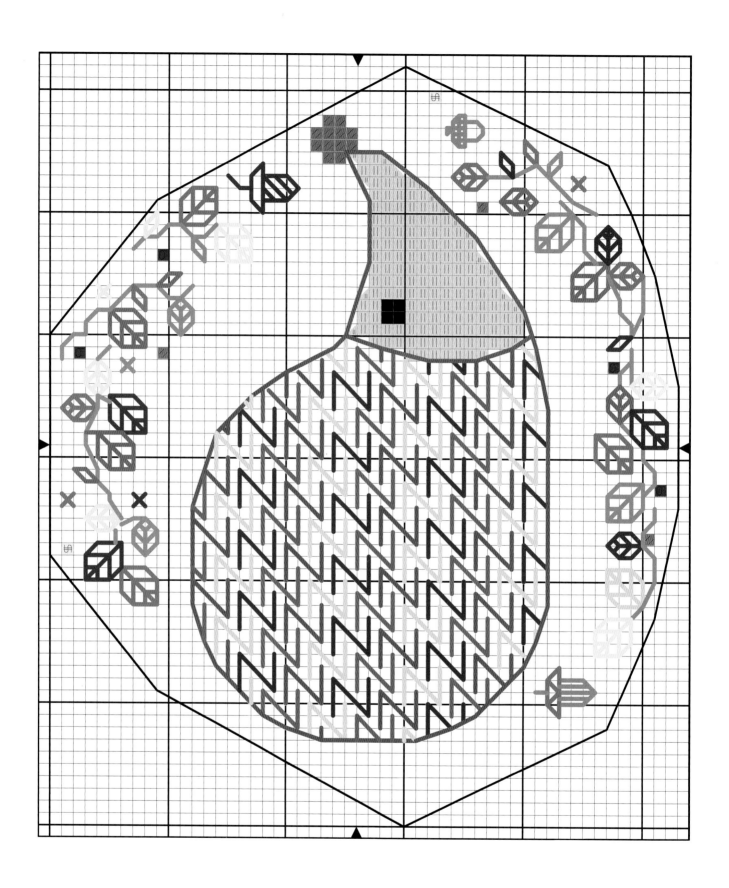

Hedgehog purse, see page 68

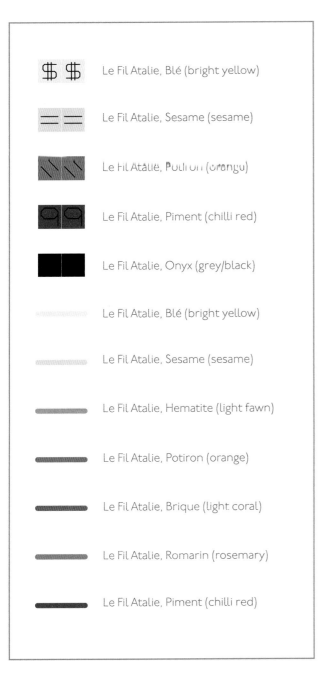

Le Fil Atalie, Blé (bright yellow)

Le Fil Atalie, Sesame (sesame)

Le Fil Atalie, Potiron (orange)

Le Fil Atalie, Piment (chilli red)

Le Fil Atalie, Onyx (grey/black)

Le Fil Atalie, Blé (bright yellow)

Le Fil Atalie, Sesame (sesame)

Le Fil Atalie, Hematite (light fawn)

Le Fil Atalie, Potiron (orange)

Le Fil Atalie, Brique (light coral)

Le Fil Atalie, Romarin (rosemary)

Le Fil Atalie, Piment (chilli red)

Note
The black lines on the chart are to help visualize the edges of the purse when it is assembled.

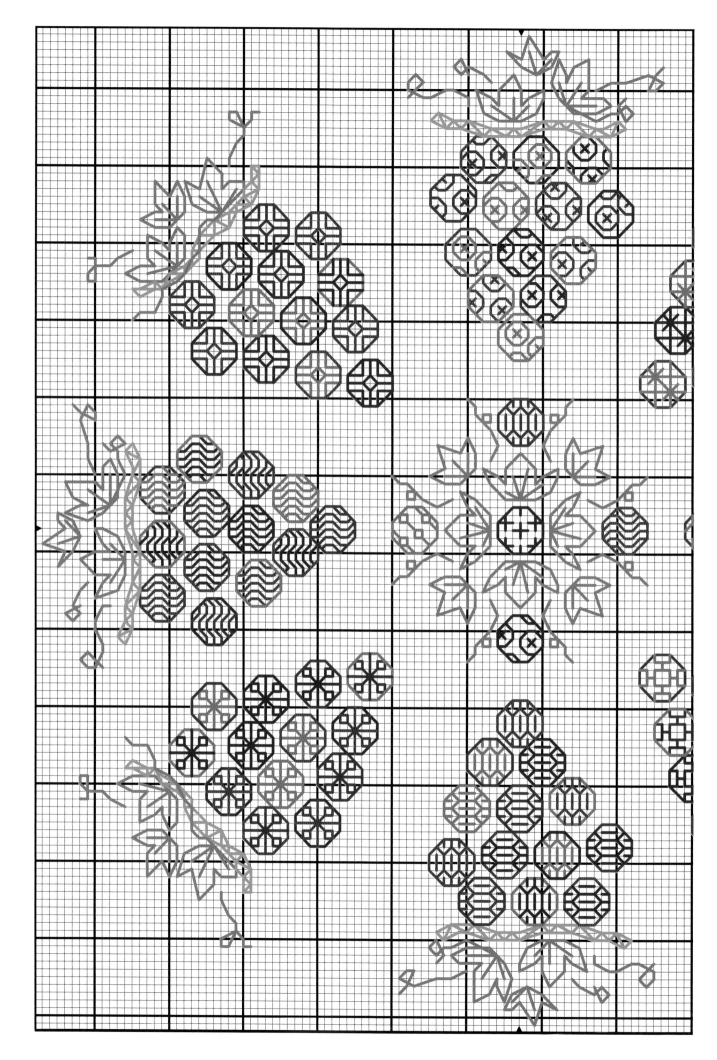

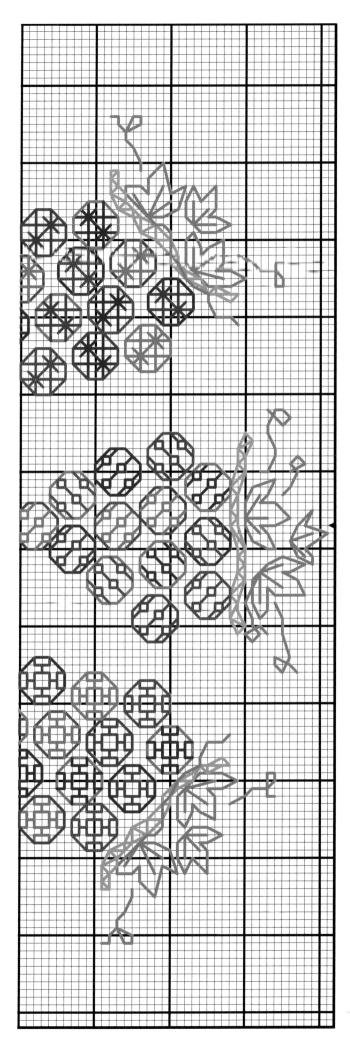

Autumnal grapes, see page 72

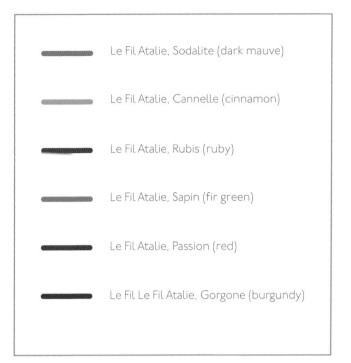

Le Fil Atalie, Sodalite (dark mauve)

Le Fil Atalie, Cannelle (cinnamon)

Le Fil Atalie, Rubis (ruby)

Le Fil Atalie, Sapin (fir green)

Le Fil Atalie, Passion (red)

Le Fil Le Fil Atalie, Gorgone (burgundy)

WINTER

Tree of Life hoop, see page 76

♡♡	Le Fil Atalie, Passion (red)
✳✳	DMC, Blanc (white)
	Le Fil Atalie, Moutarde (mustard yellow)
	Le Fil Atalie, Ortie (leaf green)
	Le Fil Atalie, Potiron (orange)
	Le Fil Atalie, Sapin (fir green)
	Le Fil Atalie, Passion (red)
	Le Fil Atalie, Vert Manon (dark green)
	Le Fil Atalie, Éthiopie (dark brown)
	Le Fil Atalie, Neige (white)

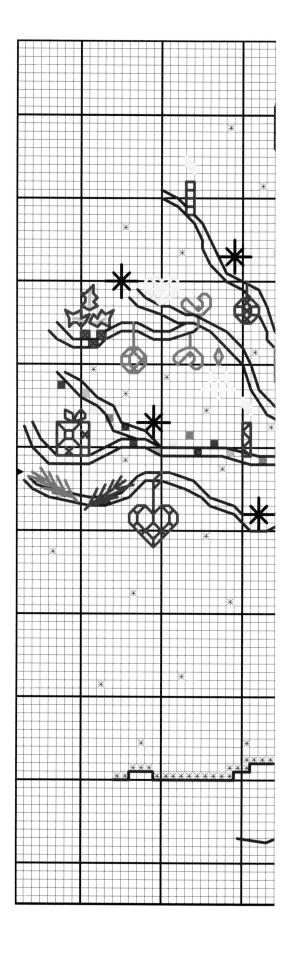

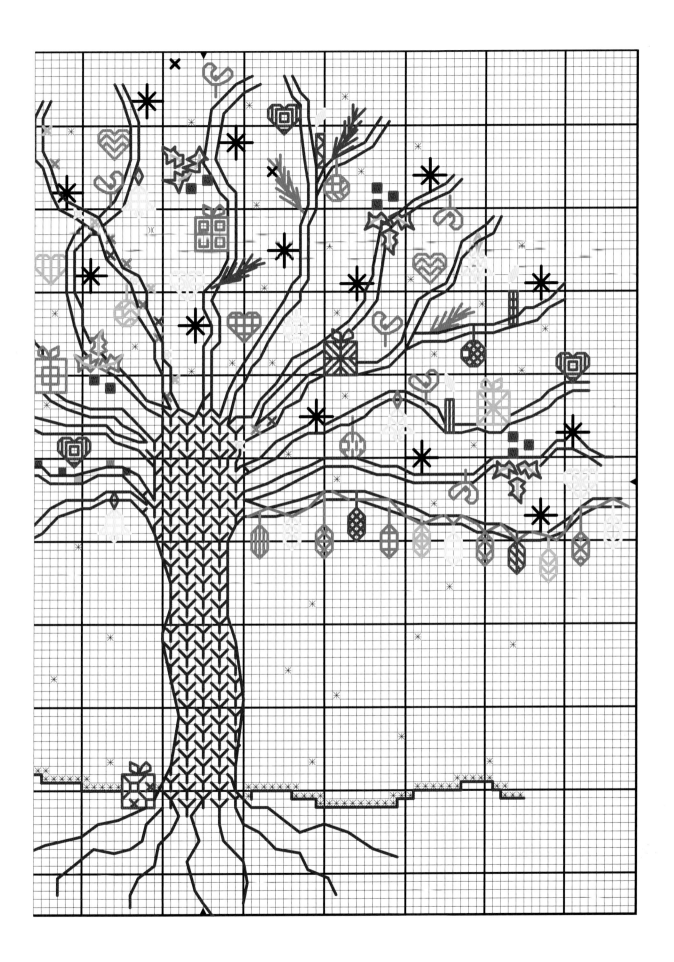

12 Christmas tree
decorations, see page 80

Le Fil Atalie,
Sapin (fir green)

Le Fil Atalie,
Passion (red)

Le Fil Atalie, Neige
(white)

121

Foliage trio, see page 84

$ $ Le Fil Atalie, Blé (bright yellow)

    Le Fil Atalie, Verveine (prairie green)

Y Y   Le Fil Atalie, Eucalyptus (eucalyptus)

♡ ♡   Le Fil Atalie, Passion (red)

——   Le Fil Atalie, Neige (white)

——   Le Fil Atalie, Verveine (prairie green)

——   Le Fil Atalie, Eucalyptus (eucalyptus)

——   Le Fil Atalie, Cannelle (cinnamon)

——   Le Fil Atalie, Vert Manon (dark green)

——   Le Fil Atalie, Passion (red)

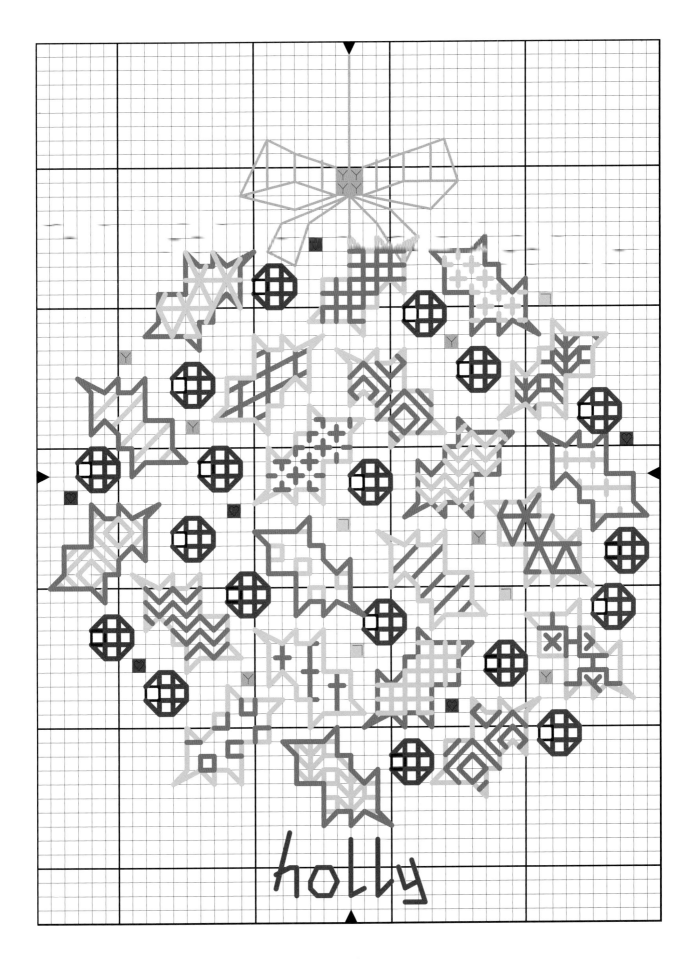

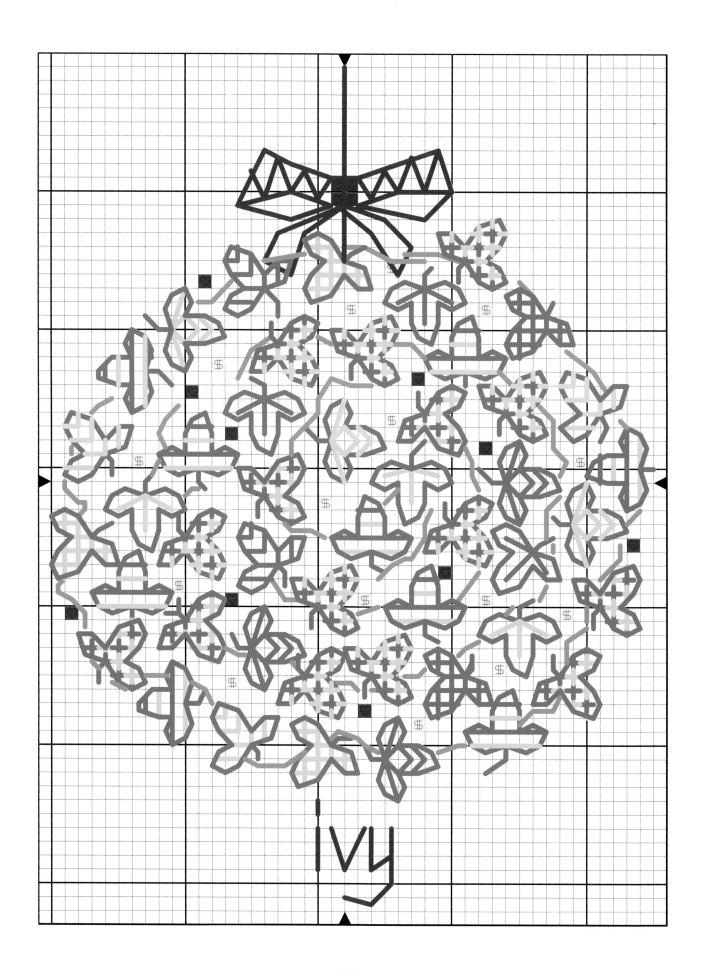

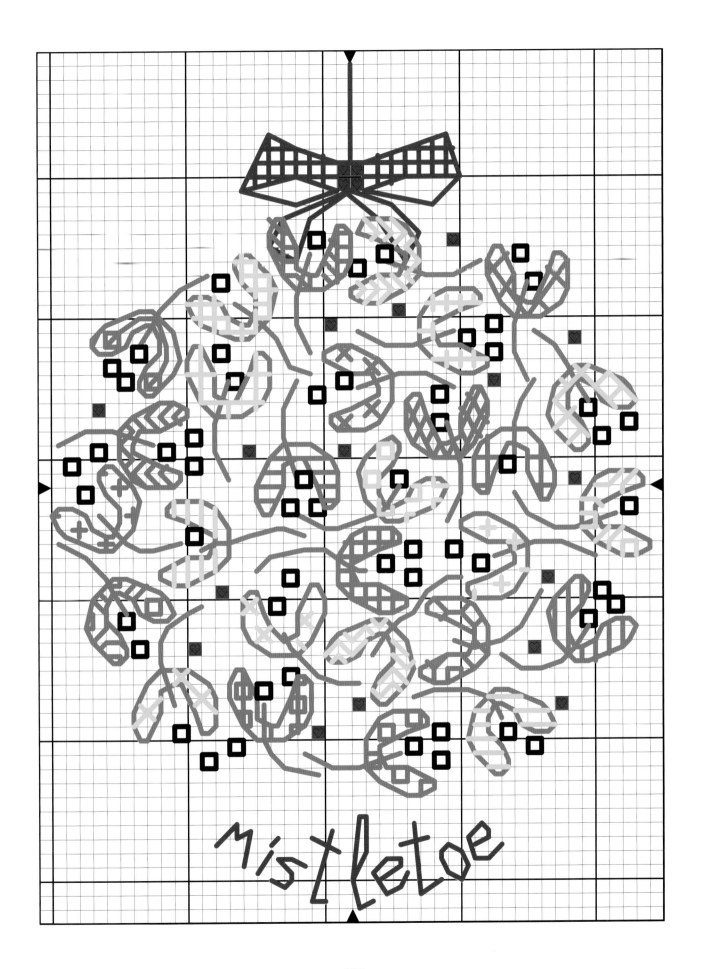

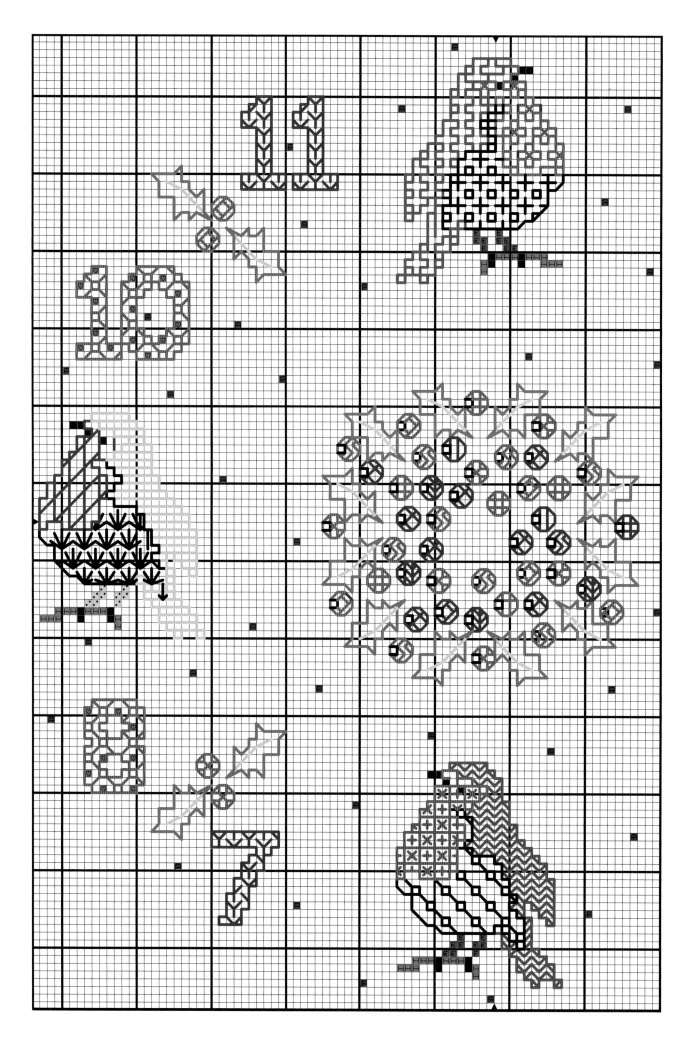

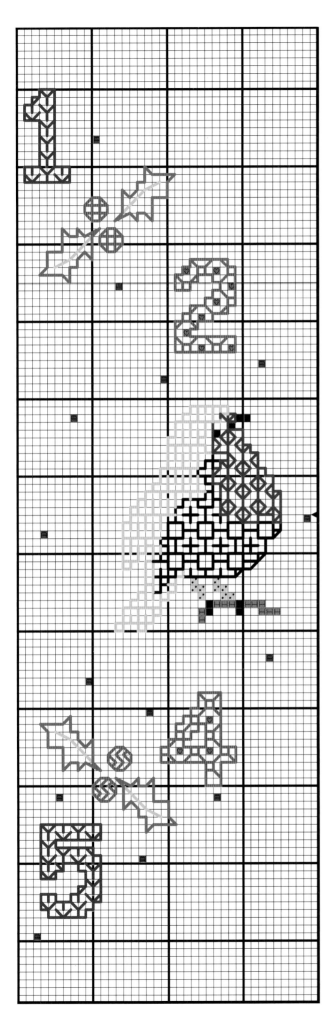

Robin clock, see page 88

Le Fil Atalie, Cannelle (cinnamon)	
Le Fil Atalie, Passion (red)	
Le Fil Atalie, Hematite (light fawn)	
Le Fil Atalie, Éthiopie (dark brown)	
Le Fil Atalie, Rouge A (bright red)	
Le Fil Atalie, Onyx (grey/black)	
Le Fil Atalie, Cannelle (cinnamon)	
Le Fil Atalie, Ortie (leaf green)	
Le Fil Atalie, Passion (red)	
Le Fil Atalie, Éthiopie (dark brown)	
Le Fil Atalie, Sapin (fir green)	
Le Fil Atalie, Rouge A (bright red)	
Le Fil Atalie, Neige (white)	

INDEX